To Melva & Mary

Raized On The Rez

Non fiction

by

Betty Jean Van Balen Ankrum

Recapture the past with me.

Betty Jean Van Balen Ankrum

Library of Congress
Catalog Card Number 96-96004

ISBN 1-57579-008-4

Printed in United States of America

PINE HILL PRESS, INC.
Freeman, S. Dak. 57029

ii

Introduction

Nellie and Van.
Magical words to a magical kingdom...of youth
They sprinkled a touch of stardust on our very ordinary lives
the fairy tale come true with a marriage
Though tragedy ends the tale
The magic of the good times radiates moonbeams
to the Lives of the survivors.

by Helen Peterson

Preface

I wrote these stories to take you on a path through past history. Hopefully, these encounters will enrich our future life experiences. These contributions came from our hearts as well as our minds. They cultivated memories of where I have been.

3 - 9 - 91

A scenerio of the Rural, Reservation, and Ranch. A wonderful way to overview the past ninety years of trials and tribulations of growing up in a changing society. Written with authentic knowledge and wit, by my daughter Betty Jean Ankrum. With my encouragement.

—Nellie Van Balen
Age 93.
Sioux Falls, S.D.

Acknowledgements

It is here I would like to acknowledge and express my appreciation to these people that so generously supported me.

Helen Kintner for offering to put it on their computer. To Dr. Roy Kintner for his expressions of value when he read some of the first stories.

To LaVeeda Wiese for her most ample, supportive, caring work.

To Mary Johnson who did hours of computer work, transposing information.

To Margy Schnell for exchanging thoughts of our families.

To Clayton and Carol Jennings who kept nudging the process.

To Helen Peterson's pictures and comments of the memories I brought to life and for her inspiring introduction.

To my family who knew it was possible.

To the Center for Western Studies for encouraging words.

To all the nieces and nephews that would inquire about the progress.

To Delores Markley and Helen Meuwissen for the pictures they shared with me.

To sisters, Molly Spain and Sarah Hofferberg, Joan's daughters, who did the cover and artwork.

To Janet Venjohn and Joan Churchman, my sisters, for the day we cataloged our thought of the past.

Special thanks to Carrie Scott for all her deeds.

To my husband (Swede), Merle, who gave me quiet time to write, shared a word when I was grasping for one and would grin when I'd say, "I'll be 100 before I finish this." Four years and ten months later, I say "finished."

Raized On The Rez

by Betty Jean Van Balen-Ankrum

In 1991 at the movie awards Kevin Costner said, "Books and movies are for things that people want to share and remember." So come sit down and I'll share my story that proves that life repeats itself with similar recurrences. This plot takes place about 60 miles from the area where Dances With Wolves was filmed on a Reservation. I can almost relive some of these rare happenings. I can articulate with honesty the experiences that taught me to love, laugh, live and trust my gut feelings. This is a tale of nurturing and serious growth. Many of the stories were told to me by my mother, Nellie, now nearly 94 years old. We shared many happy hours detailing the past, an important era handed down in these precious years. There's a lot of me in this past history. We begin this writing in January 1991.

Chapter 1

The time is late 1913. Many North European people were migrating to the United States, and with them came Joost Van Balen Blanken, a man of 16 years. Yes, I call him a man, even at 16.

He left his father, brother and sisters to follow the footsteps of his two older brothers, who enticed him to come by sending the $125 for the boat ticket to Ellis Island, New York. His father was a civil architect specializing in hydraulic engineering and the chief inspector of Dogwood, Seawall in Petten, Holland. He had a rather dictatorial manner. As a prerequisite to coming to the United State, he insisted that his son be able to speak fluent English. (Van spoke perfect English!) He was the sixth of seven children. He wanted to seek a better life. He was "hep" on career, finances, marriage, happiness, and a place of his own.

The family Van left behind.

The last time Van saw this sight—1913.

Van's point of departure.

Van's mother died in childbirth. Perhaps the stepmother who came into their family found the responsibilities more than she had bargained for when she said yes to Abraham, who had a readymade family and was lonesome for a companion. He hadn't given a lot of thought to how the children would be treated or how they would respond to their mother's replacement. For Van it was an unbearable circumstance. The strict manner of his Father was excessive. He missed the gentle touch and love of his Mother. The stepmother didn't provide that. He had fine clothes, skates, boats and guns but the difficult atmosphere encouraged thoughts of his two brothers who had already left for America.

Van was a small man, barely 5'7", born in the Netherlands in 1896, just before the turn of the century. Love and family are a reality, the reality that he couldn't live without. The prospect of going to America became an actuality. He was making plans to leave his birth place.

Van said goodbye for the last time to his family and the country that he left behind. He began his venture to America with one black pouch-type bag, a few Dutch guilders, anticipation, and courage that he could weather the week-long trip on the ship. He stood out in the crowd in his jodhpur pants, leather leggings and spotless attire. He had a gold watch that slipped into the tiny waist pocket. This watch was precious as it was given to him by his father as a going-away gift.

Many things about Van set him apart. He wore rimmed glasses, a flat-top (Ivy League) cap and a laugh that was so jovial and contagious it made heads turn and join the laughter without knowing what had been said. He knew the ABC's of life handed down by his family. Those were his guidelines to life and education. These I will tell you about later.

The trip was not without anxiety, and both a sense of adventure and of calmness occupied his mind. Knowing his brother George would meet him was gratifying. The train ride seemed long to Rock Valley, Iowa, where his brothers located and had found work. His schooling had been year around for eight years. He had taken Ag classes and had hopes of getting work with his brothers.

This would have been a very short story if it hadn't been for God's Plan. Shortly after arrival his brothers Peter and George both died, one of diphtheria and the other of pneumonia. He was not

The headstones of Van's brothers, Peter and George, in Woodlawn Cemetery, Sioux Falls.

The dairy cows.

The milk delivery wagon.

Van in World War I.

only among strangers but he had a difficult task at hand. He received some assistance and support from his cousins, the Wartenhorsts, who suggested burial be in Woodlawn Cemetery in Sioux Falls, South Dakota.

The transition, struggle for survival and homeless reality forced him to grow and mature.

You could tell his heritage when you looked at him and watched him work. There was a definite Carrel Connection. He was neat in attire, an image of Dutch clean which went with his looks. When he removed his gloves his hands resembled a professor's, and so did his mind.

His cousins, the Wartenhorsts, had a dairy business, therefore he applied for similar work at a large dairy called Lakeside. He was happy and somewhat relieved when he found work he was familiar with. The secure feeling of immigrants who were bonding and locating in one area made him to choose to stay and work on the dairy farm. Work on a dairy farm is not for most people. It is long hours. The cows have to be milked on time, with no exceptions. When the udder is full it is imperative to relieve the cow of the milk so as not to get the "dairy man's dread", mastitis in the herd. He carried out these methodical duties until World War I broke out.

He signed up to serve in the United States Army and became a medic. This suited his meticulous manner and he became a proud, naturalized citizen. He served two years in the army. Then he received his honorable discharge papers.

He was getting acclimated to the Rock Valley, Dell Rapids, and Sioux Falls area. He was emotionally and physically ready for some stability. The transition and upheaval had left his body and mind stressed. The guidance from his father was rather a big stretch away. One can only fly by the seat of his pants, so long before one lands.

6

He worked several years in the work he knew best, but he wanted a home, family, and land of his own.

The year 1924 came and so did his new opportunity. It would be a big transition and undertaking, but by now he had accumulated much knowledge and a layer of tough skin. His new job, found in the Argus Leader ads, was Dairy and Farm Manager. Again he would care for a dairy herd and be in charge of the farm. There was a drawback. The farm was in central South Dakota, not far from the Missour River, away from the cousins and other immigrants with whom he was friends. The jodhpurs and leather leggings he wore would surely be fitting because of the habitat of rattle snakes, prairie dogs and vast prairie! This job would definitely give him a broad view of life. It would be a big challenge. He was about to know comradeship not only with Whites but also with Native Americans.

In the past he'd left sea breezes and rural surroundings. He was torn by the anxiety of leaving familiar settings, but the passion to persevere and a persistent attitude to prosper had a definite grip on him. It was a focus handed down by his family: it was reminiscent of his childhood. What his heritage expected, he'd become. They were very proper and clean. What they did, they did well. For example, reclaiming their land from the sea with dykes.

It could not be a leisurely pursuit for he was 27 years old. The thought of a red-hot romance and a companion crossed his mind for the future, but such a commitment would have to be a passing thought until he was financially fit for such an undertaking. His dream of going to an unexpected place with many elements and scenes was near at hand.

He prepared his Model T for the trip. His cousins were kind and they packed him lunch and a jar of water. He bade them goodbye. Promises to write were spoken and he was off for the wild blue yonder.

His map was primitive. The sun would be to his back as he headed west for Stephan Indian Mission on the Crow Creek Reservation. At first he practiced in his mind what he'd say to the priest upon arrival at Stephan.

The clouds were beginning to look white against the blue sky and there were evidences that spring was on its way. A few flocks of geese flying north in the notorious V formation could be seen and heard. The prairie was beige and brown from winter. Trees were still barren and gray, and few and far apart. He could see the vastness.

The endless prairie was void of the fences that he was accustomed to back east. The roads were dusty in places and with few travelers.

The car got hot. The early snow thaws had left water puddles along road. He was glad he stopped and added water to the radiator. He had to be self-reliant. There weren't many places to stop. He observed the many homesteaders and a few squatters.

Time was dragging. There weren't any signs to read or radio to listen to, only the hum of the motor and the beating of the tires on the gravel. He sang as he traveled. He could see hill and dale, with varied sandy, gumbo and rich top soil. He was hopeful of the latter at Stephan.

The lunch of homemade bread, cheese and apples tasted especially good. Maybe it was because he was anxious. He checked the map, not wanting to make a mistake and get sidetracked.. Herds of cattle and sheep could be seen in the distance. He was amazed at the distance the naked eye could see from horizon to horizon. An entertaining thought said, "Do you know what you are getting into?"

He had gone too far to turn back. Besides, he was a man of his word, so there was no turning back. He wouldn't have been able to face the kinfolks he'd said farewell to. He was too proud for that. He was a man of convictions, vested in him from childhood.

The event seemed endless. The primitive bathroom facilities were few and far between. It was afternoon when he reached Chamberlain. Here he'd turn north on the last leg of the journey and new adventure. The sun glistened off the patches of ice. The barren timber looked naked without its green attire.

As he went north he was close to the Missouri River. There were more hills and trees than he'd seen all day. As he approached Fort Thompson, his eyes were focusing on a sight he'd never seen before. Tents and tepees covered a large area. The smoke rose leisurely skyward. He wondered what the tents were like inside.

The sagging, makeshift clotheslines had washing and deer meat drying. He could see that some of the meat was fresh, some was being aged. He wondered how many days it had to hang and about the dust and insects getting on it. He observed the children playing, expressing Indian mannerisms at an early age, shy and looking only with a glance at the intruder, then looking away quickly. That manner made him uneasy. He could not understand it.

The women were busy washing clothes. They were also washing and drying corn. He later found out the dried corn would be fried to

make parched corn. The families ate it between meals for snacks. Some of the corn was ground for cornmeal.

The men were standing around a carcass. He couldn't tell what animal it was. Others were cutting logs and caring for the horses. The horses were spotted, or paint pintos. The spots seemed very unusual to him, they had mini spots on the rump. Some horses had glass eyes. He wondered about their visibility compared to the dark-eyed horses. He liked horses but didn't think a glass-eyed horse would be his choice! The horses pulling wagons were mostly gray and black bay and very muscular Belgium or Percheron. They were known for their endurance.

It seemed that most of the men had several dogs, and in spite of all the barking the other animals stayed calm and unconcerned. He observed much trash and debris scattered about. He was used to clean and neat surroundings. Some wigwams had designs on them— horses, deer and dogs.

These unknown surroundings made him feel a little edgy. The sun was beginning its end-of-day escape. He knew he was getting close to his destination. He had to stop and open and close a couple of gates that had white cloth hanging in the middle of them. He found out this was so night travelers would see the gate and not injure their horses or vehicles.

A scene on the way to Stephan.

He saw a few log cabins. The toil and energy expended was evident. These log cabins had grass sticking out of the sod roofs. Crock containers were for water storage. Everything he saw had a definite purpose.

Father Stanislaus leaning on sign pointing to Stephan.

Early picture of Stephan.

He was motoring down the hill, soon to cross a creek. He was beginning to take the day moment by moment. Destiny was upon him. The sun was sliding downward beckoning its farewell to the day.

There was Stephan Catholic Indian Mission in the middle of massive prairie. The buildings were several large complexes. The American flag was just being taken down. He was reminded that he was proud to be a naturalized citizen. He was about to find out what this place was all about and what it had in store for him.

There was definitely the wooden church, but the priest's house was what he wanted to find. The bell on the wooden church began to chime. The ringing was so timely. It was his arrival and it had such a grandiose sound. His emotions were making his adrenalin flow and his heart pump hard. He put his hand to his chest to silence the pounding, as if to let his body know, "I think I'm going to enjoy the challenges that come with these new surroundings."

He found the house that he believed was the priest's house. He knocked and was invited in by the housekeeper, a tall slim lady. She disappeared to get Father.

The room he waited in was rather dark with conservative furnishings. He could hear voices and footsteps, and in a moment Father Pius appeared, the older person who had the upper hand in final decisions, and Father Justin. Father Justin was somewhat

11

Camera not focused correctly in early days—they were on way to church.

younger, with a welcome gleam in his eyes that Van appreciated. Their handshakes had a real meaning, a feeling of welcome. They showed joy at his arrival. He said, "I'm J.J. Van Balen, you can call me Van."

They all sat down and the housekeeper appeared and asked if anyone would care for something—wine, water, or coffee. The choice of wine was made by Father Pius. Van was happy for this choice when he felt the soothing effect and began to relax.

The bell rang again to give notice of day's ending and to give thanks for it. The Angelus was said and supper was prepared. Van was invited to come to the dining hall. Several feet from the building the heavenly aroma of good food and baked bread reached his senses. He was soon to find out that the nuns managed the food preparation, the bakery, and care of the children. He appreciated their talent when eating the delicious evening meal.

The dining hall was very large. Now he saw Indian children once again. Age groups of children were separated. The dining hall was underground or garden level. The north side was children, southeast was where working personnel sat. Many of them, all ages and sizes sitting on benches at long tables. From now on they were going to be a familiar sight. He began to ask questions in regard to

12

the children and their families. He learned that when they came in the fall, some would have head lice, tuberculosis or scurvy. He knew from his medic studies that scurvy was a disease of inadequate diet. His job would make the children healthier and happier. He would provide them with whole milk, cheese and eggs. He related to being away from one's family and had compassion on them.

They talked about the purpose of the mission and how it was supported. It had been started in 1886 under the auspices of the Bureau of Catholic Indian Missions. This was before the Battle of

Father Justin and Indian friends.

Sitting Bull, before the division of North and South Dakota, and during the time that Northwest Railroad was being built to Pierre. It was a Benedictine facility overseen by priests and sisters. Some children came from Brule, Ogalalla, Rosebud, Bell Court, Fort Yates, and Devils Lake, North Dakota. They were Lakota, Dakota, Sioux, Cheyenne, and Chippewa. They were from the Standing Rock, Lower Broule, Cheyenne and Northern Pine Ridge tribes, with a few Navajo from Montana and other reservations.

He was surprised to find out that Stephan put out a Woopeedah (thanks-and-joy) letter once a month to benefactors with the mission's "must have" and "needs" list. They sent it to a large circulation of people, mostly easterners and Canadians. These people gave so willingly and supported this mission almost totally. It was a heart-touching, begging letter. The lists of all items needed was usually long, with specific sizes. It was mind-boggling to think of all necessities and the cash needed to operate a benevolent mission like this. The job of the office girls was preparing this letter that the Priests wrote, opening the mail, and writing Thank You letters. They were busy. At this point he was unaware of the deluge of

13

freight that came on the railroad to the Highmore depot for the mission, and he'd oversee that too. The priests didn't speak of that task right then. Plans for that future topic would be discussed tomorrow, on a new day. They would show him around at that time.

He was shown to a two-room apartment which he was going to call home. It was located on the north side of the large building. It was not a room with a view! He began to put his belongings away. A feeling of winding down came over him. He had no problem falling asleep.

He awoke early. He had been conditioned by his childhood to be an early riser. Today he would begin his commitment to the new job. It began with the nourishing food, then the tour.

The kitchen was close so they started there, a few committed persons, some lay people. Sister Anastasia in the starched white habit came forward to be introduced. She was smiling and sweating. The fresh baked breads filled the kitchen with tantalizing fragrances. The shiny, stainless steel surroundings were putting forth wholesome beneficial food and it was warm in there. The large walk-in cooler didn't seem to have much milk cooling and he asked about that. The herd of dairy cows was very small and the milk was almost rationed. He took note of that. He would give that immediate attention. He knew the importance of milk and the many uses for it in drinking, cooking, and baking, and he knew its important nutritional value.

The dormitories housed the students. The smaller children had one for the girls, and one for the boys. The older children also had separate dorms.

The Benedictine priests and sisters he'd met were very cordial. He liked their warm, outgoing manner. He knew there would be triumphs and disappointments. Now he was ready for the full pursuit of caring for the dairy and the farm. There was several sections of grass and farm land he'd also oversee. When they went to the barn he was expecting a barn with milking machines, holding tanks, center alleyways, and tracks to make cleaning the barns easier. He was slightly dismayed by the make-shift, small, dark facility when Father Pius said, "We wanted someone with knowledge and understanding of the dairy business to help us build a new barn."

He had never guessed that they didn't have a modern barn. He was rather astonished at the thought of hand-milking cows for a school of that size. His former style of daily activity would need a few changes. He could not determine the best solution for this particular circumstance immediately but he would solve the problem. He wanted to make an effective decision. He now knew why the school was short of milk. The cattle for milking were not the high-production type. He began to wonder how much the volume could be increased if they were milked three times a day. That could be the alternative. He would get the data on current volume. Could the schedule be worked with those involved? He began to approach the decision with the question of what's best for the children. He wanted peace of mind that he was doing the best job with the personnel and resources available. This was a time when something had to be tried. The two men that would help him, both had nicknames, Pudgey and Chink.

He tried not to torture himself with what he was used to. He shared his idea with the Benedictine priest and found him generous and eager for results.

Apprehension yielded in about two months and one could see a distinct difference in the children's conditions. Their hair began to have a lustrous chocolate-brown hue. Their eyes were bright and shiny. Their health improved and so did their study and work habits. They seemed happier.

Several high school boys helped with the milking and were learning physical work and responsibility. Van was gaining dignity and respect. What society had expected, he was becoming. He was here for success, happiness and peace of mind. He was advancing confidently in the direction of his dreams. As he began to succeed, he welcomed each day from sunup to sundown. His personality was not a laid-back one. He had a sound mind and body and overworked both. The people who came into contact with him were captivated by his smile and his jovial laughter.

His daily activity schedule was showing a need for changes. The milking at 4 a.m., noon, and 8 p.m. was fulfilling its purpose, but there was no time to undertake the planning and building of the new dairy barn, silo, slaughter house and chicken house. He knew the late spring should be action time for all of these projects, and spring was upon them.

So spring came to the mission. The prairie was beginning to show glimpses of green tint. The wild crocuses were springing forth. The unique, purple wild pasque flower was seen in the pasture making its early ascension to the not-so-colorful surroundings. It was so dainty, fragrant and short-lived. Pheasants were nesting and so were the other native birds. The spring thaw, creeks were running and one could hear the rushing water bursting against the creek banks as if it were in a hurry to get somewhere. Cows, sheep and horses were giving birth to new life. As one absorbed all these miraculous happenings, one understood that the elements of God were presented. People seemed busy but happy as they went about their daily endeavors. The west was built on Spirit, and the sensation and motion of it could be felt enveloping all of life.

Van made plans for the dairy barn with cream station. He wanted the unit to house twenty cows at a milking. His motivation for action and achieving the completion was that the hand-milking routine would be exorbitantly time consuming when the school was out and his student help went home.

With this mind set, he approached Father Pius with the barn plan. He wondered if he'd have to wrangle over the plans which had all the modern conveniences, including a large silo for feed storage, a chicken house, a slaughter house for butchering meat for school and a shop for repair.

The outcome, before support of such a project was given, needed only his detailed information as to the value of such a project compared to their need. Actually, Father Pius was rather aloof about the building issue, but Van was concerned about measuring

Newly completed dairy barn.

16

New barn destroyed after another storm.

Many buildings demolished.

up to his expectation. Father was realizing Van was authoritative and believable and had great true grit, spirit and devotion, which he carried out with clever, timely comments. He gave his approval.

Frank Hawkins, a construction contractor from Highmore, was going to build the much-needed buildings. He was a good-natured man, and when you dealt with him your mind could be at ease. The end result would be perfection. He instilled pride in his employees, and he managed them well. The crew worked rapidly.

The footings were down. It was getting very cloudy on June 14th, 1924. The wind was rapidly changing direction to the northwest. Though only 4:30 in the afternoon, the wind was imprisoning them. The evil darkness was engulfing the earth. A loud roar was heard, like a locomotive. Someone yelled, "Storm, run for cover." The angry winds were lifting items airborne. Boards were disappearing. The hallowed wooden church was grabbed and squeezed by the cyclone wind and then relinquished in sad disarrangement. The fateful event happened so quickly and dispirited the mission. After the disaster, for a few days there was dismal despair. But no one was injured. A few miles away a young woman, Mrs. Peck, was killed when a board hit her in the back.

Another church would be in the making soon. There would be much to ask for now. It would take preference over the chicken house and slaughterhouse and shop, since this was a religious, devoutly spiritual-minded mission and the church was attended by students, staff, and the area's Indian and White families, central to the life at the mission.

The daily activities busied the minds, bodies and souls of those at the mission. Summer was giving way to fall and the return of the children. Country schools were in need of school teachers.

Chapter 2

Nellie Dougherty was a school teacher with a teaching certificate and three years' experience who was ready to use her knowledge. Her parents, Jim and Hannah Dougherty, moved in 1909 from a village in Kinsman, Illinois to Rock Rapids, Iowa because of the availability of the land which was very fertile. The farm they bought a short time later was at Junius, South Dakota. Nellie's education was received at country and Catholic schools until she went to Madison Normal Teacher's Training. She taught at Junius, Orient, Chester, and she was applying at Stephan Rural School. She thought it went wonderfully well. The school board was impressed with her fresh, proud and gracious manner and with her questions. She was competent and qualified. The many grades she'd have would be a challenge. The Gallagher's offered to board and room her but she'd have to walk a mile and a-half to school. The walk would be through sloughs and reeds with no paths to follow.

Her eagerness and zeal went astray the second week when the students asked if she'd seen any prairie rattlers on her walk to school! She gave a loud wail and asked if she could ride double on a student's horse.

That night she told the patrons she was quitting. They suggested she go to the Stephan Mission and ask Father Pius if she could room

Nellie when she came to the Mission.

19

Nellie and some of her students.

Nellie learning to ride.

and board there. She went that evening. In her mind she was wondering if this country was too tough for her.

Father Pius wanted good to come of her teaching choice. He encouraged her by charging only $10 a month for room and board. She would be breaking bread with the mission staff and walking only a short distance to school. She moved to Stephan that very weekend.

The air was getting crisp and light was beginning to descend into darkness earlier each day. She was grateful for indoor plumbing and a large furnished one-bedroom with a sizable closet. She didn't have a lot of clothing, just a few well-chosen items. They were feminine, soft and powerful—wool skirts, a beautiful pink cashmere sweater that made her look admirable.

The next morning she was anxious and apprehensive about going to the dining room. She dressed and primped longer than usual. She knew she'd be the center of attention once she entered the dining hall. Her stomach was begging for breakfast.

She paused, then walked in.......the tall, buxom, black-haired, green-eyed Irish schoolteacher in her fitted fire-engine red dress. She looked professional, effective, soft but frilless. Her face was ablush. She had a tender, squeezable expression. She smiled at the mass of students who were whispering, giggling and eating. Then she acknowledged the adults at the long breakfast table.

The food was definitely of country flavor with steak and eggs for breakfast. She'd never eaten steak and eggs at dawn.

The mystery was over. This was Nellie Dougherty, the new country school teacher. The office girls were ready and willing for conversation. Nellie was rather shy but a gleam of a smile melted over her lips as she was introduced to all the entire working staff. The women at one table: Mildred Schuester, Helen Herring, Elizabeth Lila, Delores and Jerry Foerster, Mary Ellen Hayes, Mable Werdel, Mary Hardes, and Kit Holtzman. The men at another: Albert Holtzman, Clarence Kuper, Bud Krautbauer, Art Meuwissen, Richard Holtzman, Emmet, John, and Mark Durfee, Ray Hammes, and J.J. Van Balen.

Van found her fascinating and pleasing to the eye. He was realizing there was more to breakfast today than eating. He couldn't remember a breakfast he'd enjoyed more. He hoped this was one memory that wouldn't fade. Her Irish charm intrigued him. The elements and scenes from the day became a distinct ice breaker for conversation during the happy social mealtime. Nellie was enjoying the fabulous flavor of the good food and had a hearty appetite like the others. The gals didn't always care for the food, so they'd hop over to the men's table and put big helpings on their plates and they'd all laugh. The men were shy, but got a "leg show" as the girls stepped back over the benches. Delores Foerster once said to one of the men, Ray Hammes, "Well look, you have one red and one orange sock on!" He responded, "Yeah, and I have a pair just like it at home!" The topic of conversation ranged from weather, mail, outings, and Ping Pong games. These broke the monotony and tension.

One evening Nellie told the others of a unique experience she'd had that day. She had stayed at school to correct papers. The children had all left an hour ago. As she sat at her desk, all at once a dead silence and a darkened shadow at the window made the school room feel dark. Her mind prompted her to look up. She looked at the window that had darkened. There stood an Indian staring in at her. She wished she wasn't where she was! She was overcome by fear. His hands surrounded his face as he stared through the window. She froze in an owl-staring position with her brain racing for "what to do." In a blink, her life could be different forever. Her desk had little for self-protection—a protractor in the desk drawer was all she could think of. She was mentally praying and asking God to intervene.

Her faith was perhaps her saving grace. He turned to leave. His hair was shoulder length and something was in it that looked like a feather dangling. He wore a fringed vest; the rest of his body she could not see from her sitting position. She noticed that he made a skyward motion with his hands. She found out later that he was a man who could not hear or speak and had been passing by on his way to the mission.

After this incident Nellie no longer spent late hours at school. Her after-school work, correcting papers and making lesson plans, was done in her room at the mission.

Everyone shared the day's events at the dining table. To Nellie it was thirty minutes of wonderful adult conversation. This social companionship, along with the beef, bread, soup, and milk, were a fixed affair she looked forward to. The group was full of vigor. They had a couple of picnic outings down by the river. They played croquet, picked choke cherries, ate, laughed and got a jillion chigger bites that itched for several weeks.

A romance was beginning between Nellie and Van—still like a recipe without ingredients—and the discovery was putting meaning into their lives. The other workers sensed the attraction between the two. Nellie was very cautious in her manner. She knew affection was beautiful but it scared her to death. She wasn't planning on any permanent romantic pursuit in the near future, she yearned for more education.

Van had a stardust fantasy that he was hug-starved but she was holding the magnet. She was an Irish lady and he was so impressed with her morals and ideals. He wished he could dance so he could hold her close and feel her warmth. She was not a lap percher or a flirt. He would have liked her to sit on his lap and whisper in his ear. He welcomed each day they talked, smiled and laughed, and he was thankful they'd met. His days were lively and cheerful. It made his life exciting; his work was performance perfect. He had emotional fondness for Nellie, the job and this place. He was advancing in the direction of his dreams, but rather overanxious and would have to make some compromises.

Nellie was busy with school. A pie social was on the calendar to raise money for some new playground equipment. A Christmas program would be next on the agenda, thus creating a rather difficult time for the attraction. Nellie would be going home for the holidays to Dell Rapids. While there she'd help her parents, Jim Doughetry's move.

The dang banks were loaning money rather easily to invest in farms if one had a partial payment. Immigrants were doing that and so were Nellie's folks. Interest was 4%. This seemed like an avenue to get a start. They invested their savings in a farm. Lo and behold, in October the Federal Reserve Board demanded full payment. The family lost their holding and had to move to a house.

Van gave tremendous effort to upgrading the dairy herd. The buildings were such comfort and work savers. He knew he needed the Friesian cows. Those white cows with black spots were known for their large volume of milk. They would surpass the present herd. The three milkings that were imperative now could change to a two-milking routine. It would take effort and records.

He made inquiries to local farm folks about a need for a mission cream station. He had a visit with Father Pius. This element would bring a cash flow. He bought the equipment and the plan was soon initiated. The cream was trucked to Highmore and shipped by rail to the Lakeland Dairy in Sioux Falls. For a time Highmore was the biggest shipper of cream on the railroad.

The farmers milking and selling cream had money to buy groceries and other necessities. The station and store got to be a special gathering place for getting to know the neighbors, discussing economics, conditions in general, and for exchanging a joke. The resourceful idea was well received and helped people overcome their doldrums. It was the week's entertainment and verbal release. They told each other what was on their mind. Repeat customers were a sign of growth and responsibility. Results come from thoughts; the cream station was a good thought and the store expanded to supply a greater variety of home items.

The road construction, though slow, was a continual process. The graded roads were being graveled and a network of fine roads was being proposed. The program was proceeding slowly but it was heartily received by the vehicle traffic. Radio sets were making their initial appearance. These early sets were not too dependable. They had a lot of static, and there was not enough power from the stations to outlying areas.

Nellie was realizing she wanted to further her education at summer school when school was out, so her romantic attitude was changing. Her heart was set on a three-year certificate so she could teach in town. She would be going to school in Madison for some classes so she could teach in town.

Van was beside himself and dealing with his sad feelings. He would dearly miss the charming Irish schoolteacher. They would discuss their future later when they could review it after a less emotional time. It was as if she were putting the future boss on hold. They would stay close by correspondence and occasional trips back and forth. If the romance went astray, it wasn't meant to be. Van was saving money and working for future needs.

The demand for farm products was increasing. The locality was especially adapted to raising livestock. There was an abundance of water and a soil condusive to raising alfalfa and other ensilage crops suited to dairying. This was a branch of agriculture that was becoming of great importance to the state.

Van was burying himself in his work. He would step up the production of corn, oats and numerous other crops. The price of these commodities was advancing from year to year. The chief cause of this rapid rise in value was the withdrawal of all free government lands from settlement on the old basis. Another cause was the increased production per acre due to better methods of tillage, a more thorough knowledge of fertilizers and more careful selection of seed.

The population of the country was increasing. The value of land was destined to increase from year to year. The increase in value of the land led men and women from the city to invest in and occupy farms. The rural area was becoming a site for very competitive farmers, all wanting to be the best producer per acre. Van didn't want to be outdone. The cream station was where they exchanged ideas and information about how many bushels per acre the crops made.

The government was offering valuable information from the Department of Agriculture at Washington free of charge. The experiment station was also at their disposal. They would analyze soil, advise them on combatting diseases of plants and domestic animals, and how to exterminate insect pests. They were constantly studying to improve the condition of farmers. Blackleg was a threatening disease that wiped out herds. Then there was anthrax, the animals were burned to take the germ out of circulation. The water holes and creeks were thought to be the means by which the disease was transmitted. The animals suffered with high temperatures.

The financial risk of running a farm is always an interesting thought. Moisture conditions, pests and prices are stresses that bring lines to the face and acid to the guts. Those that love the country become obsessed with it and overcome obstacles and griefs. The exposure to nature and its effects create an undying magnet. It was not long before farmers and ranchers began to see the value of facts which science was slowly discovering.

Some poultry was found on nearly every farm. Many raised chickens for the meat and eggs. Women seemed to get drafted to that duty. The chickens seen would be large Red Bufforington, Plymouth Rocks or white leghorns. They seemed to have free run of the farmyards. The early-morning crow of the roosters was a dependable alarm. They began to crow at the very break of day and didn't stop until they had everyone wide awake and working. Many crowing roosters were threatened at dawn with mumbles of, "We eat you for lunch, cock!"

On August 24, 1927, South Dakota was claiming the beginning of the greatest thing of its character in the entire world. The beginning of the magnificent Mount Rushmore. Gutzon Borglum began his endeavors to fulfill his vision of putting the faces of the famous presidents on the mountain.

The curious visitors traveled on the dangerous dirt trails in the Black Hills to see the proposal and view a faceless sight of the memorial of Washington, Jefferson, Lincoln and Roosevelt being carved. They rounded steep corners and backed down sloping hills to allow cars to pass. Many cars overheated because of the altitude and design of the engines.

It was the Badlands and the Black HIlls that would be the future anchor to the state's tourism. It had a beautiful setting with pine trees, hills, mountain and brooks—a perfect vacation site for families from near and surrounding states.

The trains were the major means of transportation. The mile-long grain and coal trains would rumble and clang across the vast, wonderful prairie. The hobos would be hitching rides and walking on the top, hoping to get to the west. The train engineers were unable to discourage the illegal hitch hikers. The whistle of the train was heard far off in the night. In the depot were the sounds of the Morris code clicking information to the depot agent.

This was a place to feel, hear and understand the changing west. People went there out of curiosity to see who and what were coming and going. The interest never faded, the Easterners in their proud attire were eye holding and fascinating. Van would pick up the freight at the depot, large packages he'd deliver to the second hand store which Lucy Sargeant managed. She picked out all the items usable for the mission. Sometimes she gave Van a sack of things he might like. Others could buy garments and household items that the mission didn't have use for.

Van was definitely feeling the distance and the widening gap between himself and Nellie. He felt it was risky, and he was constantly dealing with what to do. He was in the Christmas spirit. He wanted to share the holidays with her. He found a beautiful Christmas card and sat down to approach the life-changing question. He put the powerful message on the card....."My heart, mind and body ache for you. Will you be my Christmas bride?"..... There it was on paper. He mailed it and wondered what the response would be. He had dreams and hope for a future, some time a ranch in that area.

Three days later he was injured in a farm accident. His shoulder was dislocated. He would not be up to the daily activity of milking and work. He asked Father Pius for a few days off and caught the train, destination Montrose. He left Stephan a single male. The tormenting shoulder was just part of his agony. Her answer to his question, would it be glee, relief, everlasting happiness? Or would she send him back? He put that thought away.

During his 4½ hour train ride he gazed at the mostly barren fields and pastures. Touches of snow here and there. The grinding sound of the rolling wheels against the steel rails echoed in his thoughts. He kept going over in his mind whether she would have the letter and he wondered if he had asked in a proper way. Would she be happy and surprised at his unknown arrival? He tried to sleep but his body and mind acted as if they were on a high. People around him were eating sandwiches. He could smell mustard. Some were smoking, some chewing or cracking gum. Out of the corner of his eye he could see a lady redoing her makeup and primping. He thought about how he'd persuade Nellie, or would she be ready for togetherness?

The weather was cold and there was a slight wind. The train was slowing down for his destination of Montrose, a Catholic town where Nellie had twenty-five fifth and sixth graders. She enjoyed teaching in town. He picked up his bag and, holding himself as upright as possible, he stepped off the train. His shoulder ached and so did his heart.

He was happy and excited as he passed the meat market. The smell of cured meat reached his nostrils and he began to be rather hungry. He saw a cafe and considered stopping, but thought food could wait. His steps quickened and he smiled at even unfamiliar faces. Would Nellie be home from school? He'd know soon. It was 5:30; a clock had just struck. This hit him as an honest human experience which had him excited, anxious and very nervous. He had no one to vent his anxiety, about this consuming love.

The smoke from chimneys and fireplaces left little gray designs in the dusk sky. Walking up the steps, he wondered if his and her life together was about to begin. He knocked and waited. He was so anxious that he could hardly keep from trembling. The door opened. There she was—pretty, with a little smile. She opened her arms. The look in their eyes was that of mutual love. Her face and lips felt warm to his cool lips. The hugs were rather difficult with his injured shoulder. He was receiving relief vibes. He forgot about the empty feeling and began to be happy and asked for the answer to his question—the one he'd written in the letter. His persuasive manner was working. His apprehension was uncalled for. She would come to the part of America that he enjoyed: decency, honor, a clean-cut style of morals and dedicated love. He would be alone only a few more nights.

Her smile lighted up as she said yes to him. They discussed their wedding day. He had only a few days off work. She was Catholic and he would join the church. That he would do for her. How pleased she was. She did not want a divided family. Worship was very important to her Irish heritage. What would they live in? She was under contract until school was out at Montrose.

She prepared oysters for stew and had a glass of dry white wine, tangerines and fancy bread. Perhaps it was the holiday season that also nourished their excitement. Here was the person for him. What would it be like? He looked at her, there was a celebration atmosphere enclosing them.

They were busy getting the marriage license and waiting for the blood test results, and he was getting to know all the family and friends. She was so proud to introduce him. They shopped for Nellie's trousseau—satin and lace and lovely intimate apparel.

In three days they were exchanging vows in a priest's house in Dell Rapids. Because Van wasn't a Catholic, they could not marry in the church. By noon they were heading for Sioux City for a honeymoon. The wait was no more. Such a happy festive time. Van wanted this night to be at the height of exceptional love delirium. The glass of wine as setting fire to the honeymooner's needs. Van was setting his glasses aside. He was beginning to remove the jacket, then his shirt and showing his physique. She was struck by his touch. They talked in whispers to each other about this long waited arousing love venture. Always before there was moral boundaries. He was not experienced before. He fought to control himself. The endearing honeymoon began. They shared their love, ate and stayed up late talking and laughing about people and places. The

The newlyweds.

28

fireplace burned out but the loving time would be everlasting. They would begin a new day tomorrow.

The chauffeur who drove them was knocking on the door wondering when they wanted to return to Sioux Falls. He seemed in a hurry to get home. Snowflakes outside were floating down on this day of love and beauty. The affectionate time had tired their bodies so that they didn't care to hurry back. They felt the weariness of the week but really wanted to hang onto the exhilarated time. Van wanted food before the journey, and perhaps a little tour of the town. The river town with riverboats captivated their interest.

When they got to Nellie's parents' house later in the day, there were congratulations. Well-wishers shared in the joy of the new couple with their gifts. Hannah had homemade bread, pies and wonderful food for all. She liked Van. Van told her parents he'd join the church and have a house built by the time her school term was out. He'd been saving money for this new life they'd share. He'd contact Frank Hawkins, the contractor and friend who built many other buildings there and see if he could build them a house in the spring.

Van was happy to have a family here, and enjoyed getting to know the sister and brother-in-laws and Nellie's parents, Jim and Hannah Dougherty. One evening they went to the famous Palace of Sweets to have dinner in downtown Sioux Falls. It was a very updated place with marvelous entrees and high calorie dangerous dessert choices. Nellie had on her new black crepe dress with red and cream color satin tucks and bows. This was a dress you could imagine her doing the Charleston in. She had the bobbed haircut and high-button shoes and long necklace. They took her twin sisters, Monica and Veronica. They were in awe and so happy to get invited along. They had never gone to a fancy restaurant. They were only twelve and had never had such a formal meal, in all its courses and beautiful table setting. They wondered why so many forks and spoons! Van told them they could choose anything they'd like to eat. They were price-conscious and ordered beef. Nellie asked them not to cut the crust off the bread.

When they left for home, Van whistled songs. They were amazed at how anyone could whistle so beautifully. He learned that as a child and was so skilled. To them it was an unknown art. Moonlight and Roses, Among My Souvenirs, and Barcarole.

When the trip was over, Van said, "Nellie Van Balen, are you happy?" She replied, "We'll never love anyone else but each other."

29

The twins laughed and clapped. Tomorrow would perhaps be another fun day with the new brother-in-law. Veronica wished she could wear that dress of Nellie's when she got big. She knew she too would look tall, refined and keen.

The next day they discussed what they'd do for home furnishings. There was much to talk about because of no phones and no more vacations to see each other for several months. Letter writing was their means of communicating. Nellie liked mohair davenports and tapestry chairs. She would be looking at the furniture stores in Sioux Falls and saving money for the next several months to purchase her chairs. They both were happy and optimistic about their future. But the days together were over for a time. It was sad, but they had hidden hope for their future.

They said good-byes with outpouring emotion and glazed eyes. They knew the past days were actuality for new beginnings. They wrestled with the final farewells. Her cheeks were wet as she hugged and said, "I'll come for you when school's out." Soon he missed her.

The trip for Van back to Stephan seemed short. He fell asleep from the monotonous noises and motion of the train. What he longed for he had—a wife—and in the future a family, perhaps. He would push his limits for both.

Nellie had a surprise when she got back to school. The set of the World Book Encyclopedia had arrived with ten books of information and knowledge for her to explore while she digested the newness of being Mrs. Van Balen and married to the leading man with a perspective of open roads and green lights.

With enthusiasm and great motivation from his new commitment, Van went to contact Mr. Frank Hawkins. They had a mutually respected friendship. Frank kidded Van about being starry-eyed, which was a fair assessment. He gave him good options and prices: $2000 for a two-bedroom house with full basement, sun porch, kitchen, dining and living rooms, and one bathroom. He said the price would hold if they had time for wine on occasion. They shook hands. That was the contract.

Frank liked to reach out and work with Van. Both gave loyalty to the task at hand and tried to outwork one another. They didn't need a badge to say leader. It took one to know one. Their friendship was open and generous and they had joyful confidence in each other. They enjoyed conversation, work and jokes. The house was to be finished by May 15th. Frank cautioned him that two bedrooms might not be big enough. "You can have a baby a year, you know." Becoming a parent isn't everyone's dream. He didn't have doubts about raising kids. It would take very serious nurturing. He enjoyed talking about things he cared about. He had a perk of a job and couldn't wait to "play house" and start a loving relationship that would be a history of uniqueness. It would entail disappointments, joy, laughter, challenges, work, love, sickness, forgiveness and blessings. He had silent commentary, reliving every detail of the honeymoon and observing the lesson of mating so graphically displayed by the farm animals. He yearned for her in his secret thoughts. Chores and tasks took up the days. The time went quickly that spring.

The house built for Nellie and Van.

Chapter 3

NELLIE'S RETURN

Moving to Stephan was an easy transition for Nellie. She'd lived there before and made friends. The Altar Society held social card parties. There was a Country Women's Club of about eight members that got together twice a month to share recipes, concepts of raising kids, and showing off their clean homes and tasty sandwiches and out-of-this-world desserts. Each tried to outdo the other. They were the best cooks. They couldn't wait for the new member, Nellie, to entertain and to see her new house.

She bit off a few fingernails with that thought. She made a list and gave it to Van when he went to Highmore for supplies. The store there had the basic needs but she had recipes that called for unusual ingredients. Her chocolate roll would make her famous among them!

Perry Gallagher, one member of the group, was the family Nellie had first stayed with when she came to teach at Stephan so they were friends. Louise Hartshorn was a high-style eastern lady who was fun to look at in her classy clothes and who had a strut that was part of her. Her daughter, Virginia Bloomenrader, was talented with art and became a member later. Ida Konrad was one of Nellie's best friends, caring, kind and easy to talk to. Francis Novak was a workaholic with her huge garden and her chickens, and also a great dessert-maker who always had something to share if someone dropped in. Gin Wilson was the witty one with the latest scoop on current affairs. Mable Kusser, Perry's sister, was most often a guest and made a congenial addition to the group. Phil Konrad, the youngest member, was Ida's daughter-in-law, and the only one without children although she adored others'. Her recipes were usually salads. Lillian Kusser, occasionally an invited guest, was very happy raising a big family and made a mean chocolate cake with half-inch thick chocolate frosting. The group would always have a program, sometimes some enticing door prizes, and a nice lunch of sandwiches, fancy desserts, and flavorful coffee. It was a very congenial group of good friends and neighbors.

The family's clothing was ordered out of Sears Roebuck and Montgomery Ward catalogs. The choices were made by reading descriptions and looking at black-and-white pictures.

The renowned thirties live on through people's minds, souls and lives. There were bad years with drought, dust storms, blizzards, tornadoes, grasshoppers, food rationing and fires. These people had grit and guts to withstand the adversity. People bonded through family gatherings, church, card parties, barn dances, ball games and silent movies. Our heritage was founded by these pioneers who could weather the test of survival.

The treeless state was provided with funded programs so people would plant trees. Others helped build roads. The farmers using their teams could earn twenty-five cents a mile dragging a road. The rate was sixty cents for a man and a team of four horses. Teachers were being paid $60 a month. The jobs were gladly accepted. Where else could money be earned to help feed their families and buy needed necessities? These were desperate job seekers. The determined were incredibly hopeful. They didn't want dreams of a nice life to fade. They wanted paved roads. Gravel would have to do, better than what they had with chuckholes and potholes.

So Nellie and Van had love, determination and an association with many people. They all shared talents, neighborliness and silent courage. That strength produced character. They enjoyed unmeasurable beauty of rainbows and harvest moons, soon sleet and snowfalls.

The Fall of 1929 Nellie had a first-born, a son, Ross. My, how she adored the prize. She could make him smile and pass out hugs. They gave him ample love and attention. Nellie played with him and inspired and taught him by reading stories. Being the first offspring, a male, and also the first grandchild was rather a glorious affair. All the recognition centered on him.

His values for life started at an early age. Like all, he'd have his share of blunders in his childhood. One would think he'd be a carpenter (he'd tease his mother) by the way he'd take toy hammer and saw, then saw the legs of the new dining set. The new set had a few scars put there by him.

The dust storm of the 30's.

The trials and tribulations of the country's dusty depression lasted a decade beginning in the 30's. Conditions were deplorable. At first it was always the topic. The dust storms were dangerous and damaging. When outside, people covered their heads with a wrap—similar to nomads—to keep dirt out of eyes, mouth and ears. Windows were lined with oil cloths and rags, but the dirt sifted in through every crack and crevice forming a windrow of dust on the sill, so women cleaned constantly. The rains were sparse but gave the farmers false hope to plant. Then the heat and wind of summer destroyed the crops. The broken, parched land was beyond imagination. The entire midwestern states were on the move, powered by the wind. Then the plague came. Grasshoppers—hordes of them—hopping green creatures. They adorned every living plant, fence post and building. They smelled the grains and silage in the silos. They completely covered the outside, distorting the paint. The Sisters in their habits tried to get rid of them through prayer and with their cane brooms. It was a hopeless effort.

A partial relief from these conditions was brought about by programs that provided employment and small wages to those most in need. Guidelines and regulations determined who was qualified. Survival was the object.

The farmers' feed supply was soon used up. Their livestock had to be sold cheap—$15 a head—and shipped out. Many scrawny ones unable to survive the cattle drive were shot and buried. A sorry situation. Many people left the area with very little. But life went on and faith was incorporated into all the aspects of education and work. The ugly environment and traumatic conditions paved the way to a closeness among those who persevered, joined by hearts, hands and voices for support and stability. The family and its strength prevailed. Nellie was passing her traditional Irish-catholic faith on to the family. Van would oversee the physical work. The spiritual and physical would go together for a balance. The beautiful church, with ornate statues, stained glass windows and ceiling paintings, was where people came to pray, ask forgiveness and stand outside afterwards and share happenings, both happy and sad. The parish was rather small but very friendly. The folks were common, caring and proud. They oued and ahed over the new babies and complimented the older children on behavior and Sunday attire. The families were from a 15 mile radius; Werdels, Kussers, Pekareks, Knipplings, Novaks, Gallaghers, Oligmuellers, Singles, Halls, Greggs and Etbauers.

Van and Nellie were rooted and bound and they performed like models. In 1932 they were very happy with a new baby girl. She too was a Great Depression baby. She knows that now but didn't know that growing up. Van and Nellie were like puppets and the little kids pulled the strings. They were elated they had Ross and now Joan, a golden-brown-haired girl with a curious mind and body and a God-given art talent. As a very small child she would make designs with food on her high chair tray. Her childhood individuality with patterns was noted at an early age in her colorings and drawings. She could occupy her time using her talent and imagination collectively, skillfully and cleverly. Nellie's days were filled with Kind Kid Care.

Van was busy improving the farm. He was planting different grasses, particularly crested wheatgrass. It was good pasture, withstood extreme drought, was a winter-hardy perennial and had an extensive root system. The buffalo grass, a native sod grass, produced a heavy seed crop and helped control wind erosion. The grama grasses were used extensively for revegetation of range land and the cattle could gain on it.

The drought was a cycle that wouldn't go away. It was the mid 30's. The people strove to overcome the hardship.

Van had made contacts through friends and family in Sioux Falls and had learned that an area over by Spencer, Iowa, was taking cattle to pasture. He was moving some of the herd to that area. He was interested in improving the herd and upgrading by a purchasing a high-powered bull. The box stall that would house the bull in the barn would be steel rods from floor to ceiling. Holstein bulls, each easily weighing a ton, often had a ring in their nose. Their disposition was different from the Holstein cows. If a person stood outside the pen and mocked them, they'd paw, shake their head and hit the box stall. Entertaining but cruel fun.

The trips to Spencer were educational for Van. He bought, sold and traded Holstein cattle with other dairy herdsmen, who suggested he show some of his exceptional producers at the Spencer Fair. This was the world's largest county fair. Van did show. He marveled at all the beautiful creatures there. He won fancy rosette ribbons that he tied to the halters, making owner and animal special. He told Nellie about the garden and flower exhibits—God's garden on display, everything in a class, exhibited with stunning style. The well-made machinery was interesting and pleasing to see. He'd have some items on a want list. Chuck wagon races he'd never seen or heard of and he enjoyed them. The midway was a vision for the young who screamed and laughed, with the voice of the enticing barker sounding above their noise and the blare of the music. The train exhibit was fascinating and quite interesting to him since he traveled by train with the cattle.

Van had suffered a painful accident when returning with the cows in a railroad box car. While Van was milking the cows, the conductor suddenly slowed the train. The abrupt braking caused the cows to shift and he was caught in an unavoidable situation where the big-bodied cows were slammed against him. Fortunately the conductor hit the brake again and the animals swayed away from him and he could breathe again but he was hurting from the incident that could have taken his life. The trains hit head on. People and animals injured. The trains were damaged badly.

When he got home, Nellie got out the Watkins Salve and thanked God for sparing him and she massaged the aches and pains. The dust storms engulfed the sky and the grasshoppers devoured what grew on the land. The people had rare spirit and lived with the tragedies that at times overpowered the joy of life. The unspoken bond among the people was obvious.

The train wreck.

The children were growing. Ross was five and Nellie was preparing him for school, helping him with words. His interest wasn't with books. He was all boy, full of tricks and loving his mom's cookies. Often he'd tease Joan just to hear her cry for mom. Joan's hair was growing long. Nellie would put it in braids and bows. The sunroom was the playroom. Blocks, books, dolls, buggies, guns, holsters and toy tools adorned the room. Nellie's house was very appealing with her personal touch.

It was nearing the mid 30's and Nellie was feeling the kicks of an anxious, wild baby. She would say to Van that it must be a boy because it was so active.

Van had mentioned that he and Father had plans to go to the World's Fair in Chicago in October. Would Nellie like to go visit her parents? She would like that a lot and have a few days of help with the children. The children were so excited to pack the suitcase with their favorite clothes and toys.

The trip began and the children asked every few miles if they were almost there. They never went for all-day car rides. Finally the excitement died down and they fell fast asleep. The parents enjoyed the quiet time and visited during the cool fall trip. Nellie needed the stops to stretch and walk around a few minutes. The lunch they packed was a time passer and oh so good—cheese; jelly sandwiches; fried chicken; peanut butter cookies; and red, shiny, tart apples.

At last they could see the grandparents' house. The aunts, uncles and grandparents were watching for the arrival and were standing ready to give out hugs, kisses and growth analyses of the kids.

Then Van was off to the World's Fair by train. The days went fast with new things to see and do. The conversation was nonstop, until Nellie felt a sharp, biting pain that changed her expression and bent her torso over. She was going to change her plans for a visit with her Aunt Maime and Uncle Dan, Kate and Bell at 422 N. Duluth in Sioux Falls. She would take a rest and try to relax before the full-blown labor encompassed her body.

Her mother and her family helped to support her approaching delivery. Experience told her to expect 8-10 hours of labor. Wouldn't Van have a surprise when he came home from the fair?! He'd be telling about the dairy show. She'd be showing him the gift of life.

As the trees were losing their orange, red and yellow leaves, the faint morning star kissed the new, unpolluted, brisk October day. The alluring, innocent, anxious new life arrived. It was a stretching, active, dark-haired, dark-eyed, fine girl. She was in love with life and her mom at birth. Nellie held her and bonded while she stirred and sipped coffee. She dabbed on nice perfume before family members came to see her newest family member. They exclaimed about what a fine cuddly baby she was. At this point she was nameless and many were offering ideas for names.

Nellie had no regrets of pain or the events of the past months. She was happy and content with her healthy new child. There was no pomp and circumstance in this traditional family and no self-help books to rely on. There would be nurturing, action and achievement. The children would learn, grow and know their *roots* with love and hugs to sustain them. It would be part of the timetable of history, hope for the dawn of today and promise of a great tomorrow. Growth, meaning and changing times were ahead. Life would have lots of lessons, with stumbling mistakes for growth. Laughter would banish the hurts and chaos. The word bored would never be part of the vocabulary.

Van came back from the World's Fair rested and enthusiastic about the new arrival. He wanted to name her Elizabeth Jean. Nellie said that name was too long so the compromise was Betty Jean Van Balen.

Then Van and Nellie said farewell to the parents and the journey to their home at Stephan began. Nellie and Van talked and shared the happenings of the days they were apart. The baby slept. Joan and Ross played with new toys (yo-yo's and jacks) that they had received from going to the store with Aunt Aggie. It was a pretty fall day and a happy family together sharing a road trip.

This was the time of year for the World Series. The series lost its bloom for Stephan because the "Great Yankee", Babe Ruth, had been traded to the Braves. It was discussed and brooded about. The get togethers, wagering and sharing the event was rather sad for those adamant followers that waited for the final finals of baseball for the year.

Chapter 4

The time began to race by. The master priest, Father Pius, had become ill and had several heart problems. People didn't take health care seriously. In 1935 he passed away. He provided such strength to the Christian faith. He had much feeling for the Indians, as well as the whites. He was rich in spirit. He knew how the times were tough, with drought and hardships, and he was loyal to all. The prairie had his background, and now his body. The Indian families—the La Fromboius, Fleurys, Foggs, Walkers, St. Johns, Sargeants, Rousseaus, Grey Owls, La Roches, La Beaus, Wounded Knee, Harrisons, Touch, Withorn, Welles, Aken. Trust, Fallis, Ducheneau, Halls, Smells the Earths, Leo Walking Crane, Big Eagle-along with white families, all were sad. The priest "or" the Black Robe Father, who sent his white vestments wrinkling as he walked down the aisle, and who preached and practiced faith, left the living. They would accept his replacement but miss his powerful messages and convictions.

A Memorial Hall was built in his memory in 1937. The increase in enrollment made it necessary to enlarge the staff. Seventeen Benedictine Sisters were stationed at the Mission: Sister Theresa, Augus-

At the funeral of Father Pius, Clem Wounded Knee, Blind Willie, (he could find his way to Pierre, Fort Thompson and other places without anyone's help), Bishop Brady and others.

tine, Luke, Marmion, Mirian, Doual, Mathius, Wermers, Laveres, and others. They were committed to the care and education of the 250 Indian children who were brought from remote Indian villages. The Indian children were there by government order to get an education and to break their family traditions. The Indians deplored this movement. They remembered with their eyes the tragic scenes of the Battle near Pine Ridge on December 30, 1890. They did seek safety, ever fearful of the past. The relations with whites had been poisoned by the on going battles of the two races. The tribes were broken up in 1887. Their land was taken, millions of acres. The Reservation had been drastically reduced in size. They had no need for gold or silver. They wanted to be left alone, to hunt, eat what they brought in from the hunt, and rejoice. They did not want whites teaching their children Christian virtues nor the love of personal property. Their clothing was unique and hand sewn. No tailor would ever be able to match their talent. The culture nearly died out in 1890. The sacred Ghost Dance they believed in did not change things for them, but had given them something to hold on to. It was to release them from the white people's ways. With the hot winds, the break up of tribal land, the visions of their people going home, all became a useless

40

Mr. and Mrs. Smells The Earth.

struggle. The relationship was forever poisoned by constant battles. The wild west was conquered. The Native American land had been divided amongst the whites and their children had been taken from them to be educated by the whites. There struggles were ever useless, the hurt, grief, and unfair offenses were bound to them. It would be their home as well as school. A few ran away, only to be brought back. They were used to the freedom of the prairie, living from moment to moment with nature and its taste, touch and smell. Their faith would be their solace.

The dust storms were disappearing once again. The blue sky, sun and morning star were a cherished sight. The gloom of the past was overcome with splendid thoughts of better tomorrows.

Chapter 5

Lake Boehm (CCC Dam) was being built 1 1/2 miles east of the mission. It would be a place to picnic, fish and swim and skate in the winter. Many of the families helped with the project. The community ventured to the closer towns—Chamberlain, Highmore and Pierre—to attend matinees, shop and have lunches. Chores brought them home again by sunset. The road from Chamberlain to Stephan in August would be interesting. Snakes would be on the road. They like the warmth of the road. This area was their prime domain; hill, shale, river and brush for cover.

On the 4th of July the symbol of freedom was entertained by attending a rodeo at Fort Pierre or Fort Thompson and watching the cowboys Billy Abernathy, Bullet Wulff, Hank Fogg, and the Hall brothers spur the wild broncs to prizes and trophies. Casey Tibbs was just beginning his career. They were cheered, patted and complimented on their great riding performances. They were crowd-getters. The Indians and whites all found their spaces around the arena bringing their jugs of water, lunches and picnic.

Rarely, Nellie and Van would accept invitations to dinner and get the school girls Charolette Rousseau or Alvena Ducheneaux to stay with the children. They were grand caretakers. What a great time. They played games , could fix food, and put off the bed time a little by making tents with blankets over the dining table.

Nellie was finding her last child was very inquisitive, with a constant streak of energy. Van said Betty Jean could go with him when he went to Highmore to get the freight and take the cream, which they did four times a week. Nellie was an immaculate housekeeper and appreciated the leisure hours to prepare meals and invite guests from the office. The office girls said it was their oasis in the prairie. She enjoyed Mable Werdel, Mary Hardes, the Foerster girls (Delores and Jerry), Elizabeth Lily and Mary Ellen Hayes, Helen Herring, and Delores were fun-filled and lively. They were so appreciative of Nellie's invitations to come over. They would eat, have a glass of Van's homemade chokecherry wine that seemed to put guests in a talking mode, and they would have a great time. Sometimes they'd look at

Nellie, Ross, Joan and Betty Jean.

catalogs, exchange favorite recipes and catch up on the latest happenings. At other times they'd take Nellie's youngsters for walks or play marbles, hop scotch and checkers with them, so the whole family looked forward to the guests coming over. The office gals would have sweet fresh looks in their cotton dresses, bright nail polish and shiny curled hair. They added much life and laughter to the mission. Their walk was crisp as they came down the path to visit Nellie and Van. They needed a place to gather, talk, complain, share secrets of the work force, and relax.

On special occasions they celebrated birthdays with singing and whistling tunes. With much begging Van would sing Dutch songs in his native Dutch language. The song funfest was over. The kids were sent to bed and the adults told stories of the past. Many were unbelievable happenings.

Joan and Betty Jean were all ears to hear the adult tales so they'd sit down in their bedroom by the door and listen. No one ever knew all the accounts the girls enjoyed with their ears against the

Lucy Sargeant and Delores Foerster.

crack of the door. We were so intrigued by what we heard of the adult conversation.

The office staff spoke of the Indian children living in squalid huts and tents. Joan didn't know what squalid meant either. They had insufficient food and skimpy clothing but they were so appreciative of kindness given to them. There was the awesome story of Mrs. St. John, whose home was in Big Bend country, who had been stricken with pneumonia. Father Justin traveled the 30 miles along the river ice trail in -20 degrees below zero weather to visit her at the hospital, giving her the Sacrament of Extreme Unction. He left to go to the church to get Holy Communion for her. Upon his return several hours later, she was in a delirium. She said she saw five angels of extraordinary beauty circling above her. She died at 3 o'clock the next morning—such a happy death. Going home, the priest found it necessary to cross the treacherous Missouri River twice. As strange as it may sound, the car got stuck on the river.

This woman was known to have walked six miles over dusty trails, through sweltering heat, to church, fasting in order that she might receive the Bread of Life. She was buried at a Requiem High Mass.

It is incidents like this one of an old woman who steadfastly clung to her religion and practiced it that made the mission continue for the people who loved the prairies, river, and the beauty of the vast space and what the land provided. The Black Robes came and told them about God, school and learning changes. Benefactors donated buildings, food, clothing, teachers and all needed causes. People gave basic commitment to their faith by going to church. It was the strength for the next week. They entered to worship their God. Then departed to serve.

The cold weather and the flu caused ten Indians to die in one week at Ft. Thompson in January of 1937. Four were Catholic. The priests paid no attention to blocked roads. They would get several students to go along to help scoop. There were fourteen miles of snow-drifted prairie and deadly wind-chill. The four people who died were Frank Swift Hawk, Joseph White-Mouse, Mrs. Red Dog and a baby boy of Mr. and Mrs. Van Os.

The flu took the young as well as the old. The Agency put up a warning that no one should enter or leave the Agency unless absolutely necessary. This was intended to prevent the spread of the flu.

This was a year for tragedies, deaths and fires. As the blizzard would howl, a misfortune was taking place. The gym was on fire.

Priests, students and office employees all rushed to save the building but flames had gained a headway because of the wicked winds together with the lack of fire-fighting equipment. Not only the gymnasium but also the adjoining shop and garage were destroyed. The International truck used for hauling and a pick-up truck, used for farm work, were all lost. In just a short time nothing was left but charred debris. Many hands, faces, ears, noses and toes were frosted or frozen as a result of the hardship, which was borne without complaint. The typical Spirit continued. The day was memorable.

Two days later, as if too much is not enough, the water tower was on fire. Again, all help appeared to the area, where the wood casing enclosing the pipes leading from ground to the water tank were burning. Tormentingly high winds made the pail and bucket-hauling brigade seem useless. The vision of a waterless community overwhelmed them. As the casing cooled from the heat and fire, the question was whether they could store water for drinking before the pipes froze and burst. Water hauling would be with great difficulty in the bad weather and because of the poor roads. Would the benefactors be inspired to give funds to provide central heating and an adequate water supply? The priest had plenty of faith, hope and charity but no money. His motto, "We won't give up," gave the strength to continue and to go on a trip to solicit help for the desperate needs.

One of many buildings destroyed by fire.

The situation was deplorable. The school venture was daily in spite of large drifts of snow outside and smaller ones inside the classroom. The chalk trough was not coated with chalk dust but with snow. There were snow heaps in the corners and back of the stoves. Regulating the stoves was impossible. The children hopped around because of the cold, or they sweat and then dripped with perspiration. The school struggles were waged against great odds.

Joan and Betty Jean's favorite story was one about a newly ordained priest, Father Caperman, who St. Meinrod Seminary sent to help Father Ambrose. This young, small, jolly, lovable person with a humorous personality came newly ordained. He said his first Mass in a crude, unfinished chapel. He was a task taker, so he was going to Lower Brule for a church service. He drove his team many miles in early spring. While crossing the Missouri River to Lower Brule, his team broke through the ice. He nearly lost his life. The hardships of being lost in blizzards and working untiringly attracted the whites and Indians, Catholics and noncatholics, to love this man.

After the office girls' visit, the good-byes were said. The girls walked back to rooms behind the office. The front part they worked in. The back had 3 bedrooms and a common living room. The joy, fun and releases of daily happenings were over for now. The gathering and mentoring were a health cure for migraines, diarrhea and attitudes.

The next day, Nellie asked why we girls had slept on the floor. We could give her no reason. Throughout our lives we never forgot the living stories we heard during those years.

Nellie was a stay-at-home mom who was teaching the family that success would be in their value of themselves. The children would learn God's Commandments and to cherish great food with company table settings.

Chapter 6

THE VACATION

Van made plans for a family vacation. The children were so excited. He had a nice Hudson car for traveling. He thought the Black Hills would be interesting. They were working on the Memorial's presidents' faces on the mountain. The family planned to stop at Wall Drug, the dinosaur park and the badlands. The new clothes for the children—shorts, top and sandals—were ordered and received from the catalog. The tent, along with a large black suitcase, was put into the car with the camera, toys, food and water. The swimming suits were nearly forgotten! To wade in a spring creek was appealing to all.

They read the Wall Drug road signs along the way and played "I See." The roads were bumpy, so many stops were made because of car sickness. Each one had a turn. Nellie was convinced that when one got sick the next thought it was the thing to do also!

The day was hot, the kids were hot, but worst of all the car was hot. The exciting adventure was fading fast with the car problem. Hoping to make it into Rapid City, Van put the drinking water into the radiator. Things were just not going as planned. The

Ross, Joan, Betty, Jean.
Trip to the Hills.

47

excitement of the vacation was losing its enthusiasm. The radiator adversary was making the adventure affect all the family members. The kinship became quiet and strained. The last few miles prevented any good news. The car needed more water; the radiator had a hole. The cost of repair would press them and they would have to shorten their stay. Tomorrow would be a day to check with an auto repair shop. They would eat, rest and explore in the evening.

The fresh morning air with its scent of pine from the forest was a great refreshment to the family. The sleeping in a tent under the stars with nature's environment was a new memorable experience. Near Rapid Creek, the spectacular view of mountains and seeing some trout streams bursting with crystal clear cold water was a delight for the family. The planned strategy was to eat, then Van would take the Hudson to a repair shop. The experience of eating breakfast picnic-style on an army blanket in a clearing while the birds were singing and the squirrels were running about searching for food, and as a lone deer peered through the trees a few yards away, was a new and wonderful one for them all.

Later, the children waded in the stream, seeing minnows and snails to gather up. Nellie was taking pictures of this occasion for a remembrance. She was concerned about the issue of the car repair as she watched the children laughing, running and enjoying the outing.

Then Van returned, looking very serious. As he approached, he motioned with his hands and his soft eyes let them know the new radiator repair was expensive. He told them sadly that the outcome for them was that the vacation money had to be used to repair the auto. They had to gather their things and head home. They had very little money left, just enough for gas. Rather Bizarre.

Ross spoke, "It didn't take us long to vacation!" In the silence there were smiles of the trip that would never be forgotten.

The word acceptance took on meaning. The trip home was not by popular demand. It was part of life's journey. During the return trip everyone was quiet, sad and rather motionless. The orange sunset was fading as they arrived back home. A few inquired about the quick return. Van put humor into his answer, "We just can't tolerate long stays away, we had the excitement and enjoyment of getting away."

The dog Shep was happy for the return, sniffing and wagging his tail as the kids hugged and played fetch with him. The dog was a behavior modification pro.

Van and Nellie unpacked the car. Van said they would go wild berry picking (choke cherries and sand berries) soon for homemade jelly and wine. They'd take a picnic. Nellie prepared the children for bed, promising to read stories from the new Jack & Jill magazine. Van commented about Norman Rockwell's cover of The Saturday Evening Post magazine, which was ten cents an issue.

As the mission struggled for all the needs of the children, the tragedies were scandalously irrational. The search for good in every adversity was mind boggling. There were prairie fires, tornadoes, fires destroying buildings, and the well went dry. Those were blue days, full of worries and fear. The living souls all prayed for God's help and goodness. It was this and the love and gratitude of the giving benefactors that kept the mission operating. The Indian children put on a wonderful program at Christmas. Their families came a great distance in horse and wagons, wrapped in fur hides to stay warm. The gym would be full of people waiting for the performance and costumes. Then later they would see their drawings and art work. The girls, many in braids, wore beaded earrings and the boys, shy and polite.

Hauling coal in to keep everyone warm in the winter was a worry. The blizzards and cold weather made the mode of travel so difficult. There had to be much scraping and shoveling of snow. The pneumonia touched the mission and some who were stricken died. Winter burials were obstacles for Father Justin. It was hard to make the trip to the chapel fifteen miles away at Fort Thompson and even harder to go the twenty miles to the one at Big Bend. The bitter cold, the drifting snow and digging the frozen ground made things extremely difficult.

The below-zero weather caused the latest fire. The pipes overheated in the storage building, where the freight came in. The inadequate heating systems overheated the stove. The fire was Thanksgiving Day. The loyalty of the faithful workmen prevented the loss from being greater.

Everyone helped here—carrying coal for the stoves in various departments, sweeping walks and steps, hurrying to the barn to do dairy work or hastening to the laundry to help wash, iron, sort and distribute the clothes. The students cared for dormitories, dining room, washing windows, patching and darning, and helping in the kitchen. There was never an end to the jobs to be done each day in order that the routine could continue smoothly for so many people living and working together.

Merle

Betty Jean

The trip for freight was always something Betty Jean wanted to do with her Dad. He said if she was clean she could go. Mom would see to that, so Betty Jean was out of Nellie's hair for the day. The pickup was like a second home for Van and Betty Jean. This day was bright and sunny. They were just beginning to go north on 47. The road was gravel. The noise of it hitting the bottom of the pickup was like a constant, unwelcome companion. Along the way they saw a large herd of all-black cattle walking on the road nibbling grass on the road's edge, some chewing their cuds. The herd attracted Van's attention. He was muttering about what good quality they were and wondering who owned them. He was used to Holsteins (the dairy cows) and the Herefords (the beef cattle) at the mission. As he eased the pickup truck among the cows, trying to go through the large herd, it was interesting that their noses were dark gray and moist. They'd touch the truck. Their soft black eyes and matching hide were shiny and beautiful. Some would stop and lick or itch themselves. The cowboys were letting them go easy, like they were tiring. Van asked one of the hands whose cattle these were. "Les Ankrum's" was the reply - he was moving them because of water shortage. Betty Jean was looking at the rider who had a young, blond, blue-eyed boy riding behind him. The boy was hanging onto the Concho straps acting pretty happy to

Betty Jean wanting to ride horse, Ross holding the halter.

50

be part of the helping hands. He looked at her but kept his expression solemn. She waved her arm a little but he kind of ignored her then. Little did she know that lean, blue-eyed towhead would surface again later in her life, romancing her, sending her love letters with coupons good for a life-long love affair, writing her a poem that would make her laugh, and end up being her lifelong companion.

As the pickup passed through the herd, Betty Jean gave the shy guy a last tiny smile. The moving motion with the window down brought animal scents, the breeze against the face felt soft. Dad was saying what a sense of accomplishment this Mr. Ankrum must have with that fine herd and dealing with all the past shortages caused by the drought. Betty Jean needed a nap and a Lifesaver. When at home Van told Nellie about the herd and how land with cattle like that would be a dream, Betty Jean added , "I want a horse to ride even if I have to ride double. Please." I went with Dad nearly everywhere, as long as I was clean and my hair was brushed smooth. I skated in the dairy barn. Soon Dad gave me small jobs to do. He would say, "Here, take Lucy some milk now."

Chapter 7

TAKING MILK TO LUCY

When I was little and lived at Stephan Indian Mission with my parents and brother and sister, I had a task. It was taking milk to my Indian friend Lucy Sargeant. My dad took care of the dairy and the fields. I was a tomboy, with dad nearly every minute. We both wore jodhpurs. His were beige with leather leggings and mine were chocolate brown to match my sparkling eyes and long brown curls.

I was about five when I began taking a small pail of milk to Lucy each evening after the milking was done. Lucy was a Sioux Indian woman who was living in a one-room log cabin down a dirt road near the creek, less than a quarter mile from the barn.

I could smell the smoke coming from the chimney as I neared her gate. Often the fence was hung with thin pieces of meat drying in the late afternoon sun. Lucy lived there with Steve and their two sons, Andy and Jimmy.

Their dogs wagged their tails as I knocked on the door. Lucy appeared in her black dress, apron and beaded moccasins. Her graying hair was pulled back from her round face, braided, and knotted at the back of her neck. Her pierced ears, with their drooping holes, looked as if she'd worn heavy earrings.

With a jolly laugh she waved me in. Laughter was part of Lucy and she laughed a lot. It was part of her warm friendliness. She was open, honest and easy to like. The aroma of simmering soup filled the small dark kitchen. As my eyes adjusted, I could see the two beds, her Singer treadle sewing machine, and the square table covered with a red-checked oil cloth, set for the next meal with five places, which made me curious since there were only four in their family.

Lucy asked me to stay for supper. I told her I'd better not. My family was expecting me home.......but why the five places?? I wondered if she had already set a place for me, but Lucy said no, that it was a feast in memory of her teenaged daughter Alvira, who had died recently of TB.

Traditionally mothers and other Indian women in a family wore black each day for a year after a death. Lucy had pledged to feed Alvira's spirit at every meal. Food and water or coffee were put out on the plate. After the family meal, the food was burned or buried and the liquid poured on the ground. Her daughters hereafter ritual seemed so dedicated. The importance of their traditions were extremely binding to them.

Alvira's clothing was burned in a traditional burial ritual, transmitting her spirit to the hereafter. This, she said, was an important part of Sioux spirituality, freeing the spirit from earth's bondage. Then Lucy asked me if I'd like to be her little Alvira. She was pleasant and sweet natured. The sharing of cultural tradition brought an intentional friendship.

She was a seamstress, making dresses for my sister and me and aprons with rickrack for my mom. But it was the beading that took my eye. The beading went on cat gut thread for strength. She

52

showed me how she sewed the colored beads on miniature moccasins that could be worn as pins or broaches.

It was a give-and-take friendship that grew with each milk delivery. Sometimes Lucy listened to my stories and other times I listened
to hers. One day I went with mom to her Women's Club, and that
afternoon I couldn't wait to bring milk and tell Lucy what happened.

Mrs. Gallagher had asked me if I wanted to pick eggs out of the
nests. She promised a surprise for me when I finished. With the wire
egg basket in hand, I went to the strawshed that was her hen house.
As I entered, the hens made a clucking fuss. They hadn't seen me
before. I went to each nest and picked up the eggs. Her big rooster
was strutting around making a move to attack me. I threw a couple
of eggs at him. When they splattered on his head, he stopped being
so feisty!

Several hens were setting on their eggs, keeping them warm.
Before many more days, those eggs would hatch into chicks. The
hens clucked and scolded me as I tried to reach under them for the
eggs. I was pretty sure the big red hen would peck my hand when I
reached under her, but I certainly didn't expect what really happened. A big bull snake stuck its head out, with its tongue flashing! I
screamed in horror and ran back to the house!

Lucy laughed her hearty laugh. "Betty Jean, did you do the snake
dance?!" I told her I was sure that I hadn't done the Indian version!

Another time I told her how I had watched Steve butcher a cow.
There was a special building at the mission just for butchering and
Steve was the butcher. How fast he was! In two hours he had
skinned and gutted the beef, split it in half and hung it to cool, laid
the hide out like a blanket, salted the flesh side, folded it up small,
and tied it into a parcel to be taken to town and sent by rail to Chicago to be made into shoes.

Steve was the opposite of Lucy. He never smiled or said a word
while he worked. Come to think of it, that's how Andy and Jimmy
were too. Although they were just a little older than I was, when
they were home they just sat quietly on the bed while Lucy and I
talked.

Once I set some whips at Lucy's door, ones I'd made from young
willow trees, pulling them up and peeling off the bark. I'd forgotten
that trees were sacred to Lucy's people—a symbol of life and
growth. Lucy scolded me, telling me that now the trees would never
get a chance to grow strong or face the elements of nature. She let
me know that I had been very disrespectful to nature, which to her

53

was a grave offense. She told me that we all share the earth and that the trees are content to deal with the elements—storms, drought, lightning and the like. I walked slowly away, sorry for my behavior, weeping for the weeping willows. I still remember the lesson she taught me that day.

A few days later, I was doing the milk deed. When Lucy arrived at the door to greet me, I became aware of an unfamiliar smell. One that I was sure I had never encountered before. I asked, "What are you cooking?" YAWIPI. I waited for the translation - dog stew. My expression was one of shock. She laughed her jolly laugh. Then in a serious tone I said, "You won't take our Shep, will ya?" I loved Shep. He was a big shepherd dog. The harness maker in Highmore, Cliff Gosser, had made a harness to fit him and he gave us rides in the Red Flyer wagon. Lucy assured me that Shep wouldn't be considered for their curing ritual, dog stew. She was sewing a shroud. It was a cloth used to wrap a corpse for burial. It was very decorative with beads of blue, white, red and yellow. She was sipping coffee, sugared generously, giving her energy to do this meticulous work. I knelt down by her and showed her my snuff can with my possessions, a small rabbit foot, tiny whistle out of a Cracker Jack box and an Indian nickel. Also a rattlesnake rattle, about which she inquired. I was with Dad when we were driving on the road. It was a day in August and we were coming back from Fort Thompson. The road

Shep with wagon harness for pulling wagon, Ross and Joan.

had lots of snakes. They were sunning themselves and Dad said they were blind when the were shedding. They kept striking at the International truck. Dad shot several and gave me a set of 7 rattles and a button. The snake was seven years old. Each year they get a rattle. I almost forgot to ask her about one of the reasons I had come to see her. "I'm to inquire if you want the Hereford cow that was struck by lightning a few hours ago?" She said "No", that they wouldn't partake of meat that was doomed by the spirits. That day a big pot was simmering on the stove. She was expecting many of her people for the summer celebration. No matter when I went there, her house was neat, clean, beds made up and everything in its place.

Chapter 8

THE SUMMER CELEBRATION

One May evening rather late, the sound of horses' hooves could be heard plodding along on the gravel road, with the harnesses making a rhythmic sound as the cortege came closer. Then a sudden stillness. A loud knock and a voice broke the dead silence, "Mr. Van, we need water for our horses."

Van replied from inside the door, "Unharness them from the wagon before you give them a drink from the tank by the barn."

He didn't want a hole poked in the tank from the wagon tongue. It was Indian families coming from a distance to celebrate Corpus Christi. This celebration was so old and unique. They honored the body of Christ and portrayed the grief to the dead in celebration. The feast was started in Europe.

They were provided with milk and bread, and a huge snapping turtle which was caught in the creek was given to them for soup. They contain seven kinds of meat, they told us. They came for the

Some of those that came for the summer celebration.

Indian Congress and for the celebration of Corpus Christy. Both were summertime celebrations.

Corpus Christy (or Rogation Day) was a reverent, touching, symbolic ceremony honoring and giving tribute to the beloved dead and to the hallowed ground that held them. It would take place about fifty days after Easter. The Indian families put much energy and effort into this tradition that became common in the late 13th century.

The caravan of tribal members came in wagons, on foot and on horseback. A few had autos. They set up their stay in a large circle of tents and teepees near the cemetery at Stephan. It was a sight to behold.

Helen Herring, office girl.

The ceremony began at the church with the priest leading by carrying the Blessed Sacrament in a visible, gold, ornate vessel. The congregation that followed was all ages—a few White but mostly Native Americans—singing and praying as they walked. At the cemetery Holy Mass was offered. It was a very devotional and colorful exercise

Then they shared a meal eaten honoring the dead family members and friends. Lavish decorations, food, flowers and gifts were placed on the graves after the meal.

The rows of white crosses with dates of births and deaths gave the realization that many die as youth and in the early adult years.

The honor of Jesus and devotion to the deceased often included an evening pageant outside the cemetery. The fire would give off a native fragrance of sweet grasses and sage burning. The darkness, fine costumes and painted faces were awesome and penetrating to the soul.

The Indian dignitaries would lead the Grand Entry in impressive costumes. The dancers in their finest leather attire would publicly display personal faith. The dancing was symbolic of feet praying as well as hands and body. The princesses in buckskin dresses decorated with bright beading, elk teeth, weasel bones, and long fringe carried the eagle feather fans that they waved skyward during the heavy beat of the song. The waving sent the message to the Great Spirit.

Drumbeat motion and native language changed to a victory song in which men danced to a slower pace, the older dancers now participating. They shuffled slowly, with heads moving from side to side in the well-known scouting motion. The braves entered in painted faces, dancing to the rhythm in bustles and loin cloth, never exposing themselves obscenely.

The focusing thought was "Running Bare," and I was the little white girl. As I watched, their sense of spirit was apparent. When we walked away, a sadness of remembrance—and perhaps a new beginning—became an inspiration. A splendid tribute that few things are more important than family, friends and our dead.

So the drum beat, the hey-ya-hi-ya chant with beads and bones chattering to the music, is no longer heard since Vatican II (1963-1965). The tradition has not been observed as in previous centuries. It was a commendable observance that never escapes my recall.

Chapter 9

Weight and size was a rare discussion. We were not very observing it seems. Both Joan and I were in school but never noticed that Mom didn't have much lap for us to sit on. She didn't tell us she was with child. Back then it was very personal, it would be out of bounds to ask. The subject never arose when guests from the office came to visit. so as her due date came near it would be hard to tell, no nursery set up or baby things visible. She was planning to visit her parents who now lived at 1013 W. 5th St. in Sioux Falls. Nellie always went to her parents when a new family member was making a grand entry. She loved the social caring of her family. They didn't see each other often. A grand renewing time. She hadn't been to see any doctor. Just calculated the date. Counted back three months plus 7 days from her last cycle. But she wanted a hospital delivery as she had before with Ross, Joan, Betty Jean and now this baby. Her calculations told her around the 1st of July. The children would stay with Grandma, Grandpa, and Aunt Aggie. Two days after they arrived in Sioux Falls, on July 1st early in the morning the little blond girl arrived. Nellie seemed to know then that this living doll born during her early forties and when change of life was pressing near would be her comfort, love, and keep her young. Her family was com-

This is Janet.

plete now. Perhaps this summer she would do less canning and jelly making. Joan was learning all the maternal needs from watching wistfully as Nellie cared for the baby, ready to get a needed item or hum a lullaby to her sweet little sister that she got to hold and rock. She was named Janet, the name came from the Hebrews, Jane and John means Gracious One.

Chapter 10

The challenges and events of Stephan were never with a premonition. The weather was ominous as the evening approached. The milking was done and the cows were let out. The rain was pounding the earth with madness causing the water to raise and the banks to dislodge and move with the current. It was still raining at dawn. The

The herdsman of the dairy cattle.

outpouring drencher was causing a hazard to the Holstein Fresian dairy herd which had crossed the creek from the dairy barn prior to the high waters. By morning the creek ran swift and murky. It would be an earthly measure to get the herd across the swollen, roaring waters to the barn. Downed trees were flooding with the current. The young veteran Pat Enger volunteered to venture crossing the dangerous water to bring the animals to safety for milking. This young dude wore western attire. The horse and rider were a determined pair. He rode with a coiled lariat on the saddle horn and wore leather chaps and had silver spurs attached to worn boots. As he headed for the creek the cattle watched him on the opposite side, stirring in a nervous circle. It was an eerie situation as he viewed the sight and listened to Van's advice. By now people were gathering on the bank to see the rushing forceful water. They were watching and whispering as the horse reared up at the edge of the furious flood water. Then with a forceful coaxing with the spurs, the horse and rider lunged into the dreadful current. The force of the water was carrying the struggling horse downstream. The rider fought with a number of swear words to keep the horse swimming. The watchers were praying for God's help. The task was chaotic, the cattle were so frightened of what was expected of them. Their udders, tight with milk. It was an amazing sight to see the torment of the animals going into chest deep water and impossible to describe the raging current that was carrying the floundering livestock. They eventually conquered the current, floundering their way to the edge, trying to stabilize their bodies as they emerged. The by-standers applauded the brave cowboy hero who in midstream had to slide off the weakened horse and was hanging to the horses tail for support and safety. Close by a meadowlark sang his song. Shouts of praise drifted across from the grateful crowd that applauded him for a great sense of accomplishment. His victorious eyes expressed THANKS.

Chapter 11

Living at the Mission was like a legacy of decency, there wasn't any provocative or obscene viewing. There were many buildings, a Cream Station, and the old Flannery House that housed the working men and the store, where needed materials were collected. We thought that was Walnettos, lemon drops, marble like jawbreakers, Brown Cow Suckers, candy cigarettes and Horhound and Sen Sen candy, (it had the taste that stayed forever), and it was as bad as it sounds. Mom wanted MUM deodorant, Ponds Cold Cream, sugar and flour. Jump ropes were 15 cents. I begged but would have to wait. Both Joan and I loved to go to the second hand store in the afternoon. Indian wagons, with men sitting out front, would let us know that the Indian women would be inside. We were both fascinated with how the infants were laced crisscross on cradle boards attached to the mother's back. The woman's hands were free to look for her needs. The child could look around and feel secure. The women looked like they had layers of skirts on, and more than one shawl. Their moccasins were deerskin with pretty designs. They stayed in little groups when we neared them. The clothing they wore smelled like smoke from the open fires they cooked on. We stared at their uniqueness. I'm sure their "undertones" had comments about us.

We were happy the days the Watkins man came with his cases of liniments, cinnamon, pepper, spices, vanilla, orange nectar, healing salve, Petro-Carbo salve, fly spray, and puddings. The Fuller Brush man was another welcome sight. He had brown cases of brushes that we experimented with while he hoped for a sale. He wasn't as smooth as a talk show host but need was in his favor. Mom would offer him a chocolate drop cookie, just warm from the oven. As the stove sighed, the clock ticked on, the visitor of intrigue left us.

The book "Gone With The Wind" with facts of the past came out. This was coming and going time. Men were leaving for the war. Shortages of sugar, tires, gas, coffee, and cigarettes were rationed.

No vehicles could be bought. People love freedom so the young men enlisted to serve there country willingly.

The family was certainly growing. Ross was getting muscular, broad chested and impressively handsome. He stood tall and his western interest was in a good place. He never lacked identity. Being first born and a boy, the light he was born with outshone the rest of the offspring. Not an easy question, "But was he considered best of the rest?" That was never voted on but a fair question and a censored one. He was taking on men's work at an early age.

Joan spent a lot of time with her Mother. They got to know each others heart and mind. Joan liked the days of fancy baking, rolls that were picture perfect, cookies she decorated so sweet you dare not eat them. When she was in an outdoor mood we played with goats, harnessed the dog up or went to the barn to skate up and down the aisle in front of the milk cows, reading the names of the cows and opening their automatic drinking fountains. She read books such as *Dick and Jane, Ride, Ride, Ride, Bobbsey Twins, Jack and Jill* magazines and drew pictures. We were learning to love horses. I was never sitting around with idle hands. I was outside much of the time with Dad. I heard a lot of adult conversations. I was taught to listen and not interrupt. I played on the playground at school while Dad talked business. The Indian children would ask "What's your name-AY?" I didn't know what AY or ENNIT meant. Lucy would tell me.

Chapter 12

We didn't go to school at the Mission. We went to the rural Stephan School. It was a one room school where you could hear each grades classes, know who had their lessons, and who were good readers. Here's my sister Joan's version of the country school.

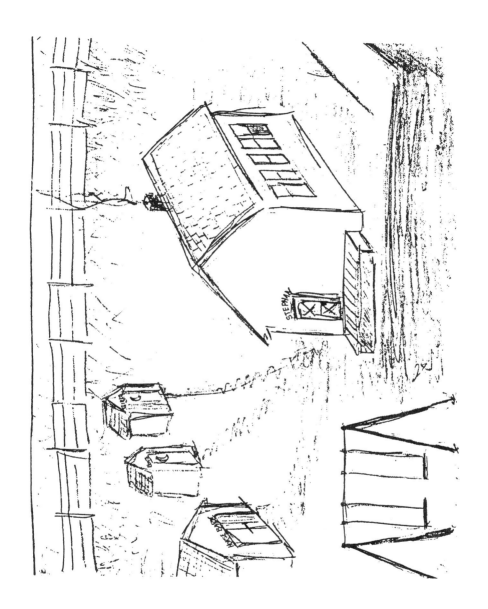

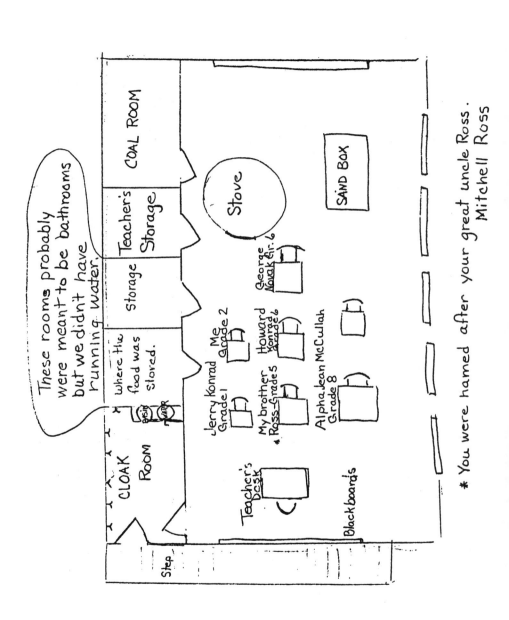

This is a picture of Stephan School. It was called a rural school because it was out in the country. Rural schools were also called one-room schools because all of the grades were in one room with one teacher. There were 6 students.

This is a floor plan of our school. The cloak room was where we hung our hats and coats and took off our over-shoes. The water cooler and the was basin was also in there. We each had our own cup. We brought our lunch. Sometimes we brought potatoes wrapped in foil and put them in the ashes underneath the big stove. By noon they would be baked.

Joan Van Balen—This is a picture of me when I was in second grade.

I grew up soon after the great depression. Some of the families were very poor and didn't have enough to eat. So the government sent food to the schools so the children wouldn't be hungry. The food was stored in one of the little rooms. Sometimes one of the big boys would sneak in and fill his pockets with prunes and pass them out to us when the teacher was looking the other way.

We lived about a mile from school. My Mom took us to school in the car. We usually walked home at 4 o'clock. When we grew older we rode our horses to school. There was a barn where we tied them up while we were in class.

We went to the toilet outside. There were two outhouses, one for boys and one for girls.

Our teacher taught all of the subjects to all of the grades. Sometimes the older students helped the younger ones with their lessons. We had art and music all together on Friday afternoon.

One day in the fall while we were studying our lessons, the sky became very dark. It looked like night was coming too soon. We went outside to see what was happening. All of the prairie was on fire, and the smoke was covering the sun.

The wind was blowing the flames away from the school so we weren't in danger. Our parents came to school early to pick us up. The fire burned for 10 miles before the ranchers could put it out. That night lots of haystacks were still on fire. It looked like we lived in the city with all the lights from the fires.

We had a sand box that was on legs. It was about 30 inches high. We made houses and trees to look like farms and cities. We used pipe cleaners to make people and glass with blue paper underneath for ponds. I liked the sand box

We played "Annie I Over" at recess. We divided into teams with one team on each side of the school. We called "Annie I Over" as we threw a basketball over the roof. If the other team caught the ball, they came around to our side and tried to tag us before we ran to their side. The game started over when all of us ended up on one team.

At Christmas we had a program for our parents and friends. We put up green sheets for curtains across one end of the school for a stage. We learned rhymes and songs. We memorized parts in plays, and made presents for our parents. Santa came with a bag of packages. Then we had a vacation.

At Easter the snow was so high that it covered up the fences. Our teacher dug a hole in the snow. She put our Easter baskets in a box and put the box in a hole. Then she covered the box with snow. We looked for them at recess and at noontime but we couldn't find them. She finally had to tell us where they were. We had been walking on top of them and didn't know it.

The End

When the days were nice we walked there through Mooneys farm yard and ganders would chase us. I wanted a horse to ride. At recess we drowned gophers, talked George Novak into riding his bike in ditches full of water while we laughed. Ross and Howard Konrad really egged him on. He would have to change clothes in the cloak room where the dried fruit rations were stored. He would fill his pockets with this fruit and pass it out during school. How we enjoyed those close quarter schools where you could pass items from student to student. That was a great little school with serious teachers that wanted you to learn volumes of information and had their eyes on you at all times.

Chapter 13

The times and happenings of prior humanity is a vanishing past. I try to unravel this like a rope and digest the synthesis for others to feel, touch and taste as I have. We have wisdom that we learned from the past. The way of life with large families is rare, as is the working together, never missing church or the social-time right afterwards. We couldn't wait for that camaraderie.

The kids planned and begged to ask if other children could come spend the day. Many times the first response would be no but after many pleases, they would approve. Lambert and Alice Knippling had many children. Their family was first a son Robert (ours was Ross), then they had Helen (we had Joan). They had Katherine (we had

Knippling family.

Anton Kos, Leonard Giever, Lambert, Jerald Knippling.

Betty Jean), then Margaret (our Janet was born later). They also had Johnnie, Francis, Carol Ann, Howard and Joey.

They had a great bunch of fun kids who were raised on milk, beef and garden vegetables. Their breakfasts were huge platters of pancakes and bacon along with four dozen eggs scrambled. The parents had many of the same disciplinary ideas. If the children got out of line, there was always yard work, raking, scrubbing floors, weeding gardens, dusting, and hanging up clothes.

The interesting and spectacular event that I attest to dramatizes the authentic west. The event was the Round-up at the Knippling Brothers Ranches. The men were up at barely the hint of dawn. They gathered around the huge oval table elbow to elbow, eating the platters of golden pancakes and crisp bacon. The fragrance of fresh coffee aroma enclosed the room. There was business conversation pertaining to the day.

The men were tall, lean and muscled. Denim shirts covered their brawny chests. Their hands were tan, warm and work-callused. The worn blue jeans were smooth on the manly hunks. There was eye contact and easy smiles toward the young girls waiting on them. The fellas controlled their urges to touch or put an arm around them while they poured coffee. They would save that for the

Knippling roundup.

Saturday night dances. The energy was there to spark a fire of romance.

They rose, crossed the room where various worn Stetsons hung in a row on the porch wall. They were off to the corrals to pick a string of mounts for the day. They would haul a load of bay, black and roan horses to the south pastures that were ten miles away. The animals were hauled to save time. The size of the pastures was

Participants in the round up.

Joan holding Howard, Katherine, Margy, Betty Jean, Johnny and Francis.

several sections of land. The horses would be well used just gathering the cattle and calves for the branding, vaccinating, ear tagging and neutering of the bull calves.

As the truck with the saddles and steeds left the chute, the sun was breaking the horizon of a brand new day. Alice began delegating jobs to her girls—Helen, Katherine and Margaret. Joan and I were guests but took on tasks too.

The food preparation was homemade scalloped potatoes, huge 10-pound beef roasts, fresh buns that were all rising on the counter, and apple, cherry and chocolate pie (two of each). Alice's little folks—Carol Ann, Howard and Joey—were waiting for food, baths and naps before they would all head out with the hot prepared meal. Iced tea was made in a cream can, beer was by the case. It was a fascinating scene.

The young brothers were teasing the older sisters about primping for the ranch hands when they were just going to the prairie for a take-out lunch. The girls had dimples and they were indented deep in the cheek when the teasing was going on.

Alice listened but never slowed her constant pace. She was a grand woman. Brains, babies and abilities were all within her grip. She gave approval for us to share their round-up. Lambert always looked at her so kindly. Such a big man. At 6'4" he was rather statuesque but those around him knew his swell manner with kids, family, friends and God. Both were humanitarians in every sense of the word. The empire they put together never went to their heads.

The bushels of food were packed and delivered to the distant corral. Here sweat and smoke from branding irons branding the young calves left an offensive odor. Those around were familiar with it all. Washing up and eating was the focus for the next hour when the men would eat. The work must not have drained their energy because they wrestled, laughed, put kids on the horses so they could ride around, and attempt to rope corral posts. Some of the horses didn't care for kids on their back and would "crow hop" and unload their riders. It was a real western sight.

The cows were bawling for their calves, which were inside the corral waiting for a roper to catch their head. Alice and Eleanor Knippling would gather the leftovers while discussing what would be the next day's menu. This energy-draining task went on for a week.

Chapter 14

Father Justin and Van discussed the work and management of the mission each morning. They were great friends and went to the World's Fair together. Van gave Father a small terrier dog for his 49th birthday which he named 49. Then one early spring day in 1943, Van was asked to come to the Priest's house. The priest invited him to the inner office. This person that he held in high esteem confided in him a conceptual escapade. He had Van as his confessor. When

Father Justin and Van.

he finished talking, Van turned and left uttering, "God grant me non-judgment, I need it." Van would carry the burden of this conversation the rest of his life. He was the person the priest chose to vent his conviction with, little did he realize the burden would cost Van his health. It was an un-called-for burden. The people knew Priests were human. If he revealed the information he would be fired. It placed a tenseness on the working relationship. He could have done without this part of American Society. He wished today would never have been. Here he was, living the mystery of faith. We have to allow room for mystery in our lives, a place where we reason, measure and grope for answers to Faith. He could use God's help in understanding his faith now. This society was never confusing before. His muscled arms, hand and body were his families livelihood. He was strong today with emotion and feelings that had accumulated here. This was a hill of history that would imprint and cause a change. Walking to his home he realized he could no longer be part of this community. He discussed the experience of the day with Nellie. He would give notice to leave. It would be a passing marker on a future change. He liked the area by Lake Boehm known as the Mission Dam which was close by. The dust storms were over and the grass was good now. The gone back acres would be tillable to raise feed. With the conversation still ringing in his ears, he decided he had no choice. He began looking for vivid descriptions of land for sale and what would be affordable. Their savings was checked and rechecked. He was a wage earner and had been a cautious spender. The find was a rather small place. A creek, that was spring fed, rambled through the land. The water level was high, so a well would not cost much to dig. The Mission Dam spillway fed the creek in the spring thaw run-offs. The stock yard would have natural drainage. Rolling hills surrounded and protected the land. To him it was going to be a new felt determination, a ranch. He knew it was right when he saw it and put his intent to buy down. He'd be a budget expert to nourish this endeavor. The house he found for $200 was small but well built. He would have to move it and put in a basement. In time they would enlarge it. The notice he gave after these past years of commitment was very difficult. He would restore his competitive zeal and rally for ranch life now. The melancholy ebb would subside. His smile would widen eventually. Maybe this change would be cause for a mask of concern to his health. Friends offered to sell him sheep. He had several horses and a pony to herd them. His children were going to be part of the work force. They would digest many experiences. He took solace that his God would take care of them. He would create avenues of income. The garden would be larger. He knew a great deal about growing plants,

This is the place that Van bought.

The ranch feed lot.

strawberries and flowers. He was a horseman and a fur trapper. Joining him when he checked traps was a National Geographic adventure. Never to break silence, following him through the snow, over stepping to use his tracks, the morning surprises of mink or muskrat caught in his traps. He would share his delight as he perceived its value.

Christmas was Van's holiday. He engineered the tree trimming, ordered Dutch pastry with almond filling and managed to find better hiding places each year. When we began to think that things were best in the winter, the snow would melt and tulips would press through the warming soil. They were the tulips that Van had planted, a love carried with him from his childhood. These too, set him apart. No other South Dakota rancher had a flower garden.

This spring a new chapter of events began. Sheep herding the new lambs on the Shetland pony, fishing the deep holes in the creek for minnows, the wild chase in the jeep after a sly fox or coyote out for their Sunday afternoon exercise. This was the same fox and coyote that would come to the gate on a cold winter night and bark its taunts and could be seen on moonlit nights on the west hill. Dad was the sly one then, for all the "Crafty" dinners were locked up safely in the barn.

74

Nellie was a great asset to Dad. She had a special touch to make the house homey, the cooking was flavorful and made for happy table time. Conveniences were easing the work, gas washing machines, gas irons and gas water pumps made household work manageable. Keeping the washing, ironing done and the little toddler Janet safe made her days eventful. One occasion Janet disappeared. Mom was frantic. Dad said we must all look carefully for her. He had been mowing. The Mission Dam was so close they were struck with fear. She was discovered later sitting in tall grass. She had followed Dad behind the mower until she tired and sat down. He never noticed her and the dust from the mowing kept her hidden.

Chapter 15

1945 WINTER STORM

The winter was edging into April; the shadow of gray clouds was appearing in the north, perhaps carrying snow flakes. Van watched the weather as it changed, sensing an approaching storm. The cattle were two miles from home on gone-back acres. Farmed prior to the 30's. During the dust bowl of the 30's this land began to blow from lack of rain and vegetative growth. Then the government had a program to re-seed it to grass. The four horses were put into the red old horse barn with the large doors. They appeared snorting, wild-eyed and rather anxious. They were given oats and hay to munch. As he closed the door, a hunch told him he'd be needing to use the horses tonight. As he went up the sloping hill to the house, the clouds looked grayer. The wind was blowing from the east. The wires were humming from the cold which he felt. It gnawed at his face. He'd listen to the WNAX station for the weather report. Whitey Larson couldn't predict whether it would be an intense storm or a flurry. Van stepped outside every few hours to see for himself. Near midnight he opened the door to peer out. The wind was more intense, the storm he had sensed earlier had arrived. He grabbed his warm clothes off the hooks. He knew he needed several riders to bring the Herefords against the storm.

He woke up Ross, Joan and Betty Jean. They got right up. Van was very tense and concerned for the safety of the Hereford cows but also about the children going out into the storm. Here was Nellie in her flannel nightie helping to dress the family warmly. They were putting on underwear, two pairs of socks, snow pants, mittens, coats, overshoes and covering their faces with scarves. As they took hold of hands to file out into the winter storm, they bade Nellie good-bye and waved at their four-year-old little sister Janet, who was peeking out of the bedroom to see what the commotion was all about.

Going down the hill to the barn, the yard light was barely visible from the blowing snow. Then at the barn door Van broke the silence with his instructions. Ross would ride his favorite, Lad, the big Palomino stallion that was whinnying a welcome to the night intruders. He was peering out of the box stall. His powerful muscles and the color of his coat resembled an animal fitting for a show stud. Joan would ride Jip. She was an eight-year-old mare that was trusting, fast, a capable carrier, and had no bad habits. Betty Jean would ride Babe, a roan ten-year-old mare. Her name didn't fit her personality. She wasn't always a Babe. She shied at rabbit holes and tumble weeds, trying to dismount her rider. Van said, "You will ride bareback since there are only three saddles."

"But Dad, I can't ride her bareback with all these clothes on. She's so big-bellied from being with foal. I won't be able to stay on if she shy's."

Van turned, a little annoyed at my concerns and spoke. "Remember that you're our rider who won the best-girl-bareback-rider contest at the horse show. If you get lost, ride till you find the fence, then ride with your right side next to the fence. That will bring you home. Ride with a loose rein."

As the saddles were being cinched snug, the sparrows flew from rafter to rafter, tweeting their disgust that they had been disturbed that night. Van and his children loved the ranch life and caring for the animals. Van was riding Lady, a fine-boned, dark-gray Arabian that showed her young age by her prance.

The group was now ready to leave the safety of the barn and the good smell of hay and venture out into the storm and darkness. They mounted up. Then they headed south, following the board fence. Then they reined the horses in a southeasterly direction. The yard light was already disappearing from their view. The lantern Van carried flickered with the wind and snow that tormented the flame. The haunting storm was friendless. A loneliness hung over the prairie and the riders. The horses' hooves made points that were covered quickly by the wind and snow. The horses seemed nervous blowing the air, making sneezing noises. A white jack rabbit sprang up almost under foot. The riders checked to see if Betty Jean was wired to her steed. Her legs were clamped like a pliers around Babe's girth.

Suddenly Van reined up and said, "Is everyone o.k.? Could you spread out a little? We should be near the white faces soon. There wasn't a harmonica tune. He started calling ca bass, ca bass, and we all chanted the words as we rode on with urgency.

The riders reached the far end of the 80 acres. There were the precious Hereford white faces up against the fence. They went in circles, determined to stay in the unsafe place. Van cautioned, "Don't crowd them or they may break the fence down. They will be goners, going with the storm until exhausted."

We carefully gathered the animals away from the fence. Van was in the lead with the lantern. The creatures began to follow the ca-boss herdsman. A young cow ran back. Ross discovered she had given birth. He got off and put the newly born over the front of the saddle. The new mother followed, bawling, very excited. The driving wind made the animals bow their heads down. They headed toward home and hearth in the raging blizzard, with an unbelievable abundance of anxiety.

The familiar landmarks had disappeared with the storm. Van's senses and the direction of the wind were his guide. The winds could shift without his realization. At times the fury of the brutal blizzard increased, nearly shutting each one off from the rest. The strange thought of loneliness was distracting but a time-passer. The heavily breathing and coughing animals were laboring from their exhausting task of going through the wind driven drifts but they never refused to respond. They sensed that nature could call death into its clutches. As they trudged on, the kids were getting stiffly cold legs and fingers. They knew the warm farmhouse would be a welcome sight. Even listening to the Neighbor Lady, Lone Ranger or Fat Man would be great. They would snuggle near the warm morning stove in the living room and the Majestic blue range in the kitchen. The gate to the corral was open as they passed through. They uttered a prayer of thanks for safety and had a sense of celebration. Nellie would have hot chocolate ready to sip along with homemade bread and jelly. The storm made hard use of the night.

As they unmounted, it felt as if they were walking on stilts with such cold legs, hands and feet. "Anyone want to Indian Wrestle?", Ross said. The girls were not game. Their ankles were frozen. They would put them in cool water soon.

The ponies were praised, watered and fed oats. Their bodies were brushed off. This would be a night to remember. The impromptu storm raged on as the weary riders noticed the turkeys were no longer on the board fence by the barn. Van and Ross began digging them out of the snow drifts. Surprisingly enough, many survived the torture of being buried in the drifts for several hours. They'd hop around in a stupor with their feathers frozen to their bodies. Some of those birds would never budge again. The barn was their reviving haven with corn, oats and water to regain strength.

As the foursome entered the kitchen, the stove's warmth welcomed them. Their cheeks were flushed. The clothes had a snow cover like four human snowmen. A fascinating sight in four sizes! Mom said they were courageous and that their endurance produced character. Tomorrow we welcome the dawn and tackle our usual tasks.

Chapter 16

It was this same year that Van began to notice a physical weakness, a disability unknown to him. His stamina diminished. The impairment was certainly related to past stress and physical drive. He had used moderation in food and drink. Only seldom the choke cherry wine would have out of bounds effect, the jovial laughter would be functioning to the hilt. The socializing was a healthy time, providing a necessary relaxed and "let" go atmosphere that was always long over due. Now he had a constant thirst that was not questioned until he seeked a doctor's opinion. The prognosis, Diabetes. He spent weeks getting used to the diet. The insulin shots were difficult to adjust. In this dilemma, Ross was forced to quit school to do the ranch work. Van went to Hot Springs Veteran's Hospital for 3 weeks to get help with his brittle diabetes. Mom didn't drive the car much, so we always rode horse to school. But not always back home. Students going out to the out house would untie the horses who would go home riderless. Mom would be so alarmed but helpless. Eventually we'd be visible walking over the hill. After a conference with the teacher, it happened less. It was quite the struggle for Ross to take over all the tasks and barely 15. He put his flesh and soul towards this big undertaking. He grew, matured and had never quittin' guts that make for surviving. In time they accumulated enough capital to buy more land and build a feed lot, shop, and cattle sheds. The house was enlarged with a modern north picture window and new Youngstown Steel kitchen cupboards. The improvements were proudly displayed to visitors.

BERRY PICKING

Picking the large, sweet, flavorful and delicious strawberries at dawn was a task we did about 3-4 times a week.

The meadow larks would perform a concert while we picked. They were definitely in good harmony as dawn gave way to a new day. We would wonder what mom was fixing for breakfast. As the sun was warming our backs, our stomachs were giving up empty pangs. We rarely ate berries as we picked even though they were large, sweet and wholesome. We would walk with a bent back after picking several flats of berries—until we'd focus on a beautiful, fragile butterfly or the morning doves and their cooing—loving and peaceful.

When breakfast was over the Nash was loaded for the trip to the Brown Derby Cafe where the berries were sold. The delicious desserts were on the menu for lunch. The groceries needed were purchased from a list at Wait's grocery store and personal care items at Casey's Drug Store.

THE RANCH LIFE

They were training us children. Life gives time and space. It was an option how you used it. Van believed we couldn't handle that so he thought up all sorts of things to fill our days. We wondered why every minute of every day we had to be doing something productive. He wanted us to see nature in all aspects, like picking strawberries at dawn. Even the mosquitoes hadn't retired yet for the day. Dad had us seining minnows in early hours before the little fish bait were fully awake. He calmed our fears of the depth of the creek Where the water runs fastest is where it's usually the shallowest. He encouraged us to learn to swim or dog paddle, just in case. Van so much believed in America and its spirit. It was nice for him to see his children discovering America. A father prepared his children for life. This cultivation came in layers and levels of work. The baby chicks were darling when they arrived in a large box. The colorful Banty's were so pretty among the Leghorns. But cleaning the chicken house, washing eggs and picking chickens were pressing burdens that were valuable, but working together we overcame these monotonous challenges.

MINNOW SEINING

The meandering creek was where the minnow seining took place weekly, despite the pleading of us girls. Getting into unknown, waste-high water that was cold in spring and mossy and muddy later, fear of snakes and bites of insects kept us from enjoying this venture! Van taunted our fear. We'd survive. We begged for hip boots but to no avail. We went barefoot and were very aware that there might be barbed wire or glass in the creek. Sometimes the thoughts of the job brought us extreme anxiety, but Van was close by giving constant instructions.

We seined against the current and were reminded to keep the lines straight up and down and move along rather quickly so that the catch wouldn't jump over the net or slide beneath. The tiny minnows would swarm ahead, flushed out of their hidings in the reeds and cattails. Iridescent bubbles would be floating on the water, giving away a telltale inkling that the fish were in that area.

The Man of War bird would be flying close by, circling, very aware of the intruders. He would make a sudden drop and then he would fly back with backswept wings. He would grasp a fish and fly up and circle. When the nets were rather heavy they had to be pulled up quickly to check the catch. It took skill to catch the bait. The energy expended made us girls wobble to shore tired, and on some occasions with leg cramps. The endurance produced character and a silent courage. The minnows were put into a screen trap along with crayfish, with their powerful pinchers.

We dismissed the small turtles. The snapping turtles were huge with a shell-size diameter of twelve inches. They were feisty and would snap at a stick and hang on. We gave those to Steve Sargeant, who dressed them and told how a turtle's heart will beat for hours after being butchered and cut up.

The fishing customers had no consideration of time. They'd drive up at 4:00 a.m., honk, then wait for a persuasive bait sales girl. Who could care about bait at that hour?! We wished them good luck, and we'd no sooner get to sleep when there was another honk. We told them we heard fish were biting in the daytime only! That fish tale didn't work.

The work left little time for games like marbles, jacks, dominoes, horseshoes, kite flying or pick-up sticks or riding to Kussers. Listening to the *radio* shows ("The Lone Ranger," "The Shadow," "Ma Perkins," "Helen of Trent," "The Fat Man," "The Neighbor Lady," "The Hit Parade") was limited and in moderation. Movies with Shirley Temple and Westerns with Roy Rogers were attended. *National Velvet* was a special movie I could relate to because of my love for horses.

HERDING THE SHEEP

Herding the sheep was a daily chore. Sheep have a nature that they want to go where they don't belong, like into a neighbor's cornfield, across a highway or into a growing crop. The task isn't difficult but it is oh-so-monotonous day after day. Joan and I took turns on most occasions. The pony was the favorite steed because we could jump off and on him easily. Before they were shorn, the sheep would roll on their backs and we had to jump off the pony and flip them over or they'd die shortly.

The closeness to nature was an education in itself. We saw the birth of life in all things. We watched the clouds change and the sky looked sometimes friendly and at other times damaging and dangerous.

This was a cloudy, rather gray, overcast morning. I was the sheep watcher that day. The sheep were moving rather rapidly to the far section. They perhaps sensed an approaching storm. Most days they grazed and the lambs played as they moved along. There is always a leader. Today the leader was a dumb, white-faced ewe. She had tasted the neighbor's corn a few days earlier and wanted to cross the highway and lead her followers to John Gross's cornfield. I was like a Miss Bo Peep who was losing her sheep, but I'd know where to find them!

The pony was not minding the bit or the commands. He kept shying at rabbits and rabbit holes. I was tormented by his manner and kicked him in the withers. We experienced the wind abruptly changing directions. The sea of green grass was thrashing one way and then another. We were reaching the far end of the pasture but the sheep were heading fast for the cornfield. Thunder and lightning were upon us. The large drops of rain were wind driven. The pheasants and prairie chickens were frightened, took wing and sought shelter near the dam. There was no shelter for horse or rider. The lightning streaked to the ground all around us. Thunder and then lightning were attracted to us. The first strike was so close that I realized the shock somewhat, but the pony continued to pitch and hurl his body onward. His feet were wet and he reacted with wild bucking as he comprehended the electricity, unseating his mount. Then he was free and running for home. The clouds were dumping water and I was getting wet to the bone, running as if my body was ahead of my legs, lightning tantalizing me. I had spirit and faith and began to pray. I said Our Fathers and Hail Marys, with promises, and asked God to help me endure the storm. When I headed west I had a glimpse of the horse almost home, and doubted that with the heavy rain coming down the family would notice the mountless horse and wonder what had happened. In perhaps record-breaking time I stumbled up the steps, fumbled with the entrance door and burst in, sliding across the black and white marbled rubber tile in the kitchen. I knew the depth of tiredness as I shook and cried out, "The sheep are in the corn and will bloat if we don't rescue them soon!" Crying was cowardliness, but I did not care that they saw me crying. I was changing, my body giving new shape, my hormones were kicking in causing weeping emotional times, which mother never discussed those coming changes with us girls.

Chapter 17

SUMMER OF 1945

The summer vacations were laced with a balance of spending some time with the Grandparents in Sioux Falls. It was an exciting place to go. The Kool Aid stands, bologna sandwiches, a place we could trim the crust off the bread, roast marshmallows in the oil stove flame, and drink Root Beer. When country kids go to town they are never lifeless or comatosed figures. They stride for parks, picnics, swimming, playground equipment at Terrace or Sherman Park, picking apples and going to the store for milk. Aunt Aggie would be game for whatever we desired in 1945. She offered the opportunity to eat lunch downtown at the Nickel Plate, then go to a movie, Colt , with Hopalong Cassidy. We would ride the bus both ways. Going downtown was pretty ordinary, as was the lunch and the movie. But the unexpected elements and scenes changed when we came out of the movie. It was VJ Day, the war was declared over a few hours earlier. The distinction was earmarked in my mind. Such provocative viewing I had never seen before. Alcohol had made animals out of humans, such hugging and kissing, and some relieving themselves. Noise, horns, bells, physical perimeters were being displayed. My fresh, proud guidelines were missled in the reckless, rebellious, celebration. My Aunt was nervous and anxious to catch the bus and get me to Grandma's house. The buses could barely get through the wild crowds, some had their hair shaking with the rest of their body, screaming, singing, passionately and performing wildly. The bus ride was some of the same. The bus driver would go by corners, lack of hearing the signal to stop. We arrived home to smell the aroma of fresh boiled coffee that Grandma made along with homemade bread and rolls. She asked how the movie was? I said good, but this day it wasn't the movie to remember but unknown behaviors.

Chapter 18

These stories are like a patchwork quilt. This one is a difficult patch. April 5, 1992. I'm putting it here because this is how far we were sharing these contributions that came from hearts and minds of Mom Nellie and I.

Here I share my recent loss, we start and end with family. Our favorite Irish woman that gave us inspiration, strong will, character, quick wit and showed us how to live a fulfilling life with zest and laughter, went to her heavenly family on April 3, 1992 at age 94. I will miss my mom, Nellie Van Balen as she is known to others. On her last day she said, "Betty Jean, get your adjectives in order." She was referring to the days I asked about the past. She interpreted as I was writing it. These grieving days caused us to reflect how we lived and loved our Mother. The outward emotion left us teary eyed and sad in spite of out faith of life after death. She was valiant, wise, up to date on current affairs and a diplomat. Grieving I find difficult and writing harder. Now I will write in memory to bring the past alive through her permeated strength. We received expressions of caring from those that matter to us. Death is a reminder of out limited time and how we want to progress with out own venture. Like a spotlight that focused on our past, it thrusts an urgency on things to achieve. The recovery of grief begins with much discussion of Nellie's personality. From here on the present, past and future take meaning. I make no apology for emotions and tears when reminders of her surface. It is the cost of love and honor of her memory. It is a sad actuality for me. She taught us to love and care and from these I live, pray and play. I'm coming to terms with the loss and how I feel stops the merry-go-round of life for a time. So lets get back on the merry-go-round and proceed. The day after her death I couldn't sleep. I was writing a tribute to her and read it at the wake. When I read it yet it jerks my emotions.

TRIBUTE TO NELLIE VAN BALEN

I was with mom on Thursday April 2, 1992 when it seemed she was reviewing her life. When she'd get stuck on a first or last name I would fill in the name she was thinking of. Then out of the blue she said, "Betty Jean, get your adjectives in order" and I said, "Now mom remember I'm not the school teacher." Adjectives in Webster's says it limits or qualifies a noun, like good, every, etc. So Saturday night I woke up and the thought she spoke came back. Was she talking about the book we were writing or about the day she gave me the ABC's of Life? Mom was a great cook. At dinner on Sunday when I was nearly eight she said, "I'm having club Friday. Betty Jean could you get me a rooster for the chicken sandwiches?" I said yes. I knew how to use the wire hook that we caught them with. After dinner I went outside rather concerned about getting the rooster by Friday. Ross, my brother, came along and he was going to ride over to our ranch east of Stephan that the folks just bought, so he said "Will you go with me?" I said, "Will you help me kill Andy the big buff rooster?" So he did, and I said we have to pick it but we put it in the garage in a pail, and off we went to the ranch to get the horses, riding through the gravel-pit, talking to fisherman at the lake and it was nearly dark when we got home. About Wednesday noon my dad came in for lunch and asked who put the dead chicken in the garage. I said, "I did, I forgot about it, and went riding with Ross on Sunday." Dad said to bury it. But that day mom and dad gave me the ABC's of Life. I spoke of these on page 2. Some related to what just happened.

A——Achieve what you set out to do
B——Beware of blunders
C——Choices
D——Is for Dreams
E——Emotions
F——Faith-Fun-Family
G——God be grateful
H——Harmony
I——Interruptions happen
J——Joke

K—Kind and caring
L—Love and laugh
M—Music
N—Never give up
O—Options
P—Pride, positive
Q—Quiet time
R—Rise early
S—Self esteem
T—Talents-we all have them
U—Usefulness
V—Values
W—When you deceive, what a tangled web you weave
X—Xcell
Y—Yearn for direction
Z—Zest for life

Nellie at age 94.

I will remember mom when I have good coffee, red grapefruit, apple pie, date filled cookies, chocolate rolls, and chocolates. She loved the grandchildren, family and friends. She loved reading the Highmore Herald and Stephan News. She liked cotton nighties and pretty blouses with brooches. My mom didn't indulge in drinking, smoking or the lottery. She had the winning ticket to God's Kingdom in the life she lived. Mom, I'll get my adjectives in order for you.

Nellie and Betty Jean.

Chapter 19

A TEENAGE STRUGGLE

The group was gathering to caravan to the boarding school. Someone asked, "Where is Betty Jean?" Joan said, "She went to the barn." So Van volunteered to get her. When he strolled into the old red barn there I was, trying to say good-bye to each of my horse friends. As I turned my cheeks were flushed. "Dad, I'm very sad about going away. I like watching these colts nudge and nibble at each other and race around the lot. Then when I get some oats they come up cautiously as I reach out a handful. The muscle on their nose tickles my hand as the oats spill out between my fingers. I will miss the fall horse sale, when you save some, but sell most. How sad a day it is to loose a favorite friend. Do you have any idea what it is like to be leaving behind the only life you have ever known. Moves are so difficult for me. When we left Stephan Mission I began chewing my nails. I know only country life. I'm going to be lost in a girls school with rigid directives. What will I do with my free time? No pets, no home life, no parents, no home cooking. I wonder about uniforms and nylons. Those leg confining hose and garter belts. You have watched me with this

Betty Jean at Mount Marty.

struggle of packing. I relate you also went away about this age. When I went to Lucy's yesterday to get my uniforms that she made for me, I told her of the agony of going away. She said it was my 'weaning time' ."

And now as tears were rolling, Van spoke. He said, "It's part of your destiny. I want the best for you." He reached into his pocket for his white handkerchief, he said, "You can do it dear."

That was quite the summer. Everything was changing. Foundations were poured for a house addition. One evening when Joan and I were getting ready for bed, I said, "I'm not riding horse so much tomorrow, it's just wrecking my rear. I have ridden so much my jeans are bloody." She looked at me so serious and said, "Well, honey, your a woman now." I wasn't told anything prior about girls' bodies changing in this manner. Being a tomboy I may not have liked that information. But now I am off to boarding school and a woman.

GOING AWAY TO SCHOOL
(It was like at this place Gods were watching us)

School was a rigid structure of the St. Benedict order. The bell rang for rising and mass. The students and the Sisters lined up in the hall, then filed into the chapel. The Sisters stood with their hands chastely folded beneath the long black scapulars that covered their floor-length, fitted black

Students in dining room at Mount Marty.

89

garments. They recited the Divine Office in Latin. The students, in white blouses and navy blue jumpers, were less taken up with prayer so early. They tried to make eye contact with the altar boys, who were attired in snowy surplices and trying to appear angelic The Smith boys, Jim and Joe, were freckled and butched; Mike Wermens was curly and shy. The Donahoes, Jerry, George and Jim, were sober; Tom and Bob Binder, Jack and Frank Lyons gave serious image that couldn't be dissolved by roving eyes. They were all part of the early morning pulpit.

The order was founded by a fifth-century monk, St. Benedict, who proposed a balance of prayer, study and work for his followers. Their contact with lay people was limited. Visitors who came could sit in the parlor but never go to the monastic enclosure. The new students from various walks of life were forcing them to be available to listen and grow with the now-changing generations. The nuns were rather friendly in a cool, detached fashion. It would take time to mellow the rigid manner. The habit called for respect and little funny stuff. Most dared to smile and laugh. The way they were, would change to the way they'd become, with the changing generations.

Sept. 1949

Dear Mom, Dad, Ross, and Janet,

I know this letter is long overdue. I'm still sorting my feeling of discomfort from the transition from ranch to private school. This is dramatically different, this turmoil. I feel I'm distinct, but individualism and uniqueness is lost in the mass of students. I know you want us to catch the vision of wisdom. I'm grateful for that, but my bright spirit, freedom, and wild physical vigor feels trapped. I'm healthy, fit, but limited activity is so disciplined. You are all so far away and I long for the open spaces and family love. There is no substitute here. The breaking bread is exactly that. For breakfast it's bread, peanut butter, honey, or syrup. Guess it's better than bread and water, Yah? The dinners are sandwiches and fruit. Supper is the best food, meat, potatoes, vegetables and dessert. We aren't supposed to talk, only in low voices. I am assigned work, for the tuition school reduction. I help with the dishes. Can you imagine doing dishes for 300 people? Yikes! Sister Daniel says we have to keep our mouths shut! They are really hung up on quiet here. What a restricted behavior.

There are days I pretend to know less than I know. I'm so overwhelmed with this adjustment. I realize its a sacrifice to send us here but I'm not sure it was a good choice for me. You wanted the best education for us.

Christ is incorporated into all aspects of our education. I should grow in faith and see his presence in faculty, family, and coeds. I will acquire a Christian attitude to build faith. It won't be a hearse that first takes us to church!

I am making lots of friends. They say I am open, honest, funny, and easy to like. I was nominated for president of the Freshman class, but the nuns have a different opinion. They are trying to motivate me to their way of thinking. They let me know that they could tell I wasn't a spectator but an instigator, a free thinker, and a persistent one. They will probably get gray trying to restrict my behavior, or I'll get kicked out. In English class the assignment was to write what your book of life would include. Some wrote pages. I wrote, Freedom, Faith, Family, Friends, Fun, Love, Laughter, and Work. When I read it I smiled, laughed and said these things are making me become what I am. I should have said, "And Sister you are going to have trouble hammering me into the life you expect. My combat days are now."

I wish I was home today hunting prairie dogs or gyrating in a slow gallop with loose reins on Lady. Has anyone been riding her? Have you weaned the colts? I think I have a better understanding of separating off spring from their mothers. Within minutes the emotion begins as the gate or door is closed and there is no longer togetherness. The young colts will spend days running to the gate checking every inch for escape. The mare will agonize for a time when the fullness of her bag to nourish the colt becomes tight. She too checks the gate in hopes to get relief from the colt. I can still see them run a few feet, look back to see if the foal is following. The relentless, head out to the grass and water. I did check the door a few times when I got here. I guess I need to talk about things I care about.

Caring about you, Love
Betty Jean

PS: will write more later.

October, 1949

Dear Family,

I know you look for our letter as we do yours. The weather is changing. The winter days are approaching. The birds have gathered and left for a warm climate. The little fat sparrows are still perching on the limbs discussing bird business. Looks like they intend to weather the winter. I guess I'm weathering this school. I'm not always in step to their beat. I think my pace is rather rebellious. The Sisters will be dingy by the time they conform this energetic freshman. Community appreciation hasn't hit me yet. You taught us values and habits. Here they forget fun and laughter. I try to display this personal reflection. We had some funny encounters lately. Clarice Lawrence and I do dishes (in the silent zone). Well, we got put on the basketball team together. Sports here are very competitive and I don't like being a loser. So I said, "Clarice, you've seen the Stephan Chieftans and how quick they are, how they steal the ball, intercept and guard the players like scouts. Well, lets do that at our game tonight." We were very aggressive and a little obnoxious. We beat a very good team that had Marlene Jones, Sandy Schaefer, Detta Rameil, Eileen Huntemur, Margie Knippling, Nila Nickels, Ann Naughton and Bobbi Jo Weiland. Our team, Barbara Schramm, Clarice Lawrence, Anna Varilek, Doris Joynt, Ruth Wortman, Donna Lane, Kathleen Lyle and I were like wild robots. Some were little bitty and others reeked with refinement. The next morning, which was Saturday, while we were all in the room, we get a knock on the door and in walks Marlene Jones. She was not a good loser the night before. She said, "Betty Jean, where did you come from?" Laughing, I said, "My Mom, why?" She said, "What nationality are you?" I proudly replied, "Irish and Dutch." Then she said the most

92

maddening and undesirable sentence. "You know Irish and Dutch don't amount to much." I had been making the bed and I had the pillow ,Mom, that you made me from the goose and duck feathers. I knew I was not going to count to 10 before I responded. With more courage than courtesy, I hit her with the pillow with all the energy I'd use with a sledge hammer. The pillow broke and she stood in a cloud of feathers. Joan, Maritta and Leona Werdel laughed insanely. Shortly I could hear the swish-swish of the habit, the click of heels and knew that Sister Roswitha was on her way. I said "Help, save the feathers, I need a pillow." I knew when the door opened who it was, but she couldn't see us for feathers and giggles. Sister's quick pace caused static electricity so when she opened the door the feathers degressed on her. She looked like she was tarred and feathered! Her dimples and smile were not present. Her words were penetrating, but the laughter couldn't be hushed. She asked what had happened. I explained, "My pillow broke." Then the truth came out. Marlene Jones was a tattle tale. I got campused. I could not leave the premises for anything. Nor could I go to the little store or Bobs Cafe, which was just off the grounds to the northeast. The word Campus went straight to my brain. I had a softness and tenderness, but these disciplinary measures shielded these and deep longings for the past made daily circumstances a daily torment. I don't know if you'll understand all this but I'm paying for the happenings with Campus. YUK. I hate that choice of confinement. These walls kind of close in on me. The cleaning up took several hours, no vacuums, so when you swept it was making the feathers air borne. I thought about where those feathers had come from. That foggy morning when Dad, Ross, and Marvin Oligmueller went hunting at Hartshorn Dam. With a few shots, 80 ducks lay floating on the water. Dad came to school and got us to help pick ducks all day. The neighbors, Lucy, Steve, and us had a time picking 80 mallard ducks. We had many meals of wild duck and dressing.

I dropped Latin. I don't know of a need for it. I'm not going to be a Nun, no way. I have too many class preparations. So now I take Art, English, Algebra, Home Ec., General Science and Typing I. My Home Ec sewing doesn't look like Lucy's. I'm not too sure about typing. I have strawberry picking fingers and they hit the keys in threes. Some students are talented and make me nervous. They burn up the keys and one typewriter actually smoked. I guess I'll close. Thanks for the money. It will mold because I can't go anywhere to spend it.

Bye and Love,
Betty Jean

P.S. Next time we are home, if its a nice day, can we go to the river and look for artifacts and arrow heads and pick wild plums? We can watch the graceful deer come out of the dried bushes to the salt licks. The fawns will be loosing their spots.

Dec., 1949

Dear Family,

I can't wait. I am getting so anxious to come home for the holidays.

We got the money for the bus tickets. We will arrive about 9:15 at Highmore Dec. 21. Who will meet us?

We have been doing a few bratty things. Tuesday evening I said to Margaret Knippling, Eileen Huntemur and Marlene Jones, "Let's not go to Compline. When it gets 8:00 let's sneak down to the 4 o'clock room." That is a place to gather, talk, whisper complaints about school, drink Coke and Orange Crush and eat candy bars out of the candy machines. The idea was Okay with all of them, but when we got down to that wing of the building we heard voices of the nuns, so we had to hide in the trunk room. It was dark and musty smelling. We kept thinking someone would hear us stumbling through the suitcases and trunks and our giggling. I peeked out. Down the hall were three Sisters talking. I said, "This was a reckless idea. Let's run up to 4th floor to our rooms before the bell rings dismissing Study Hall and Compline so no one will see us." We were running fast. First was Margaret Knippling, then Marlene Jones, Eileen Huntemur and myself last. Now we were running scared, so our feet and hearts were on a dead run. Just as we got to the 4th floor Eileen fainted from fright. The bell rang and you could hear everyone coming to the dorms not far behind. Do you know what I did? I hopped over her and dashed to our room so I wouldn't get caught and campused again. The girls that arrived and saw Eileen on the 4th floor landing helped her up. She said she got sick in study hall. She's a quick thinker!

We went Christmas caroling one evening. That was fun. We rode in a big green feed wagon from the farm. The people clapped and gave us candy treats. When we got back we had hot chocolate with fancy Christmas cookies. Great Escape.

One day over the weekend it snowed. A bunch of us went out and played Fox and Goose, and made angels in the snow. The traffic stopped and watched. Guess they had never seen a bunch of girls playing in the snow. Many of them were Yankton boys.

Next year I am going to get a job downtown during Christmas shopping season so I can make some money and get out of here all day on Saturday and Friday evenings. I'm applying at Scotts Dime Store.

We went to the Opera, downtown Wednesday night. You either love it or hate it. I doubt if it gets into my soul. The fresh air and the walk to and from felt good. Lots of boys drove by us, asked silly questions. We didn't tell them our real names or ride with them. There was one I told my friends I get first dibs on. He was cute, dark haired and driving a nice car. We all giggled and decided next time we get out for one of those productions we'd spend some time primping before hand. That may cause us to be an unruly bunch. Some of us spend a lot of time together. We get to know mind, heart and manners of each other. They say my sense of humor, imagination and memory is great, and I have something planned to do, whether it is kosher or not.

We have a few basketball games coming up. Also a St. Nicolas holiday dinner. Got to go. Lights are blinking.

Anxious,
Betty Jean

P.S. (2 days later)

I and Margaret always get out on weekends if we can, but Katherine sometimes primps all day and sits and reads True Confessions and True Romances, rather provocative after pledging Legion of Decency.

We told her she sits and dreams about her boyfriends. The other day she instigated a situation and knew how to back out of it like a saint, before the reprimand came from Sister Marie. Sister Marie likes her high speed typing, leadership and the bucks they spend here. Somedays that's a slight shadow of annoyance. She's also a fabulous fine tuned flirt.

Ross I'm trying to take your sage advice, "Don't let your ass get as wide as an ax handle from the peanut butter and honey." Not many mirrors to see our physical perimeter. "Loving words Ross." Advice of that sort keeps our blood flowing, otherwise we may get lethargic. I hope I have cowgirl country buns. I'm like a race horse, ready to run home. I like the songs, "Sincerely" and "Cheatin Heart."

Love to All,
Betty Jean

May 1950

Dear Family,

I'm not only marking these last days off I'm blessing them. Joan and Leona had their Senior pictures taken at Janasheks. Gee, they both look like beauty queens. Of course they bobby pinned their hair several times and put lotions and potions of make-up on. They are acting like real dignified Seniors.

Joan Van Balen, the summer she entered Miss South Dakota as Miss BHTC.

Not much of it is rubbing off on me but Maritta

96

is shaping up. Joan says she is entering the Miss South Dakota contest when school is out. She and Sister Leonardo are working on chalk art for talent.

They had Senior Skip-Day last week and of all places, they went to the Penitentiary in Sioux Falls. That day there was a rumor that a man was loose on the fourth floor of the dorm. Perhaps a repair person. When they returned home it was near bedtime - they were on a contagious high. We were telling them about the rumor of the man on the fourth floor. Maritta said "There's good in every Adversity." We laughed about what that could mean since this was a very proper place. When things got rather quiet, Joan whispered to me, "Put your pillow case over your head and crawl over and come up by Leona." So while I'm doing this we could hear Maritta and Leona praying the rosary. They were on the third mystery when I rose up. Great Balls of Fire! There was a scream out of Leona that was similar to the coyotes when they would howl at twilight when they had their eyes on the sheep. Then a body quake of laughter. And when that slowed down I said, "Holy Cats, here comes the penguin! I'll be campused until fall!" There was another jolt of laughing and we could hear Sister Roswitha nearing. Joan said, "Maybe Dad will pay bail so you can herd sheep this summer." The door handle turned and Sister flicked the light on. I said, "These Seniors are sure giggly. Did you come to tell them Goodnight?" She was half smiling when she asked what had happened. She scorned a look when we said "memory gap." They told her while I nodded in agreement. I said, "Sister, you should live with us, then you wouldn't have to keep getting up to come over. On her way out she uttered something about wanting to convert my spirit.

Being away at school has been a hardship but we have made it a pastime of sharing episodes of laughter. Well, packing day can't come soon enough.

Wouldn't you know that about the time school is out we are meeting the available Yankton (Bucks) Boys. Clarence Courtney, Maynard Justra, Art Hasker, Lavern Stevens, the Block Bros., Jack Anderson and Harold Uhl. They flirt with us when we walk downtown. Sure makes the walk intriguing. We always stop at Walbaums for fountain cokes. Shop in Fantles. On the way back, Dyer Creamery is enroute. They have tormenting flavors of ice cream. That is where the young people hang out. We have checked out K&K and Ben's Market. At Tielke Garage we view the new autos. During the week we may go to Green house, a small house converted into a grocery store. It has the basics, bread, candy, and personal needs. Bobs Gas Station is a place some go to smoke and drink pop, talk and laugh. It is just across the campus to the north east. Sister frowns on asking to go during the week.

Bye
Betty Jean

Chapter 20

That summer was the beginning of the family changes. Joan, Helen Knippling and Betty Kusser were packing a suitcase and catching the bus from Chamberlain to Spearfish Teacher's College. I sure missed her but Janet and I became working buddies.

The sheep shearing was always a hot tiresome operation. Bud Beastrom and his brother Connie did our shearing. Janet and I were the wool trampers that year. The wool sacks were 10 foot long burlap sacks. They hung from a steel ring up in the rafters. After several fleeces were shorn they were thrown in the long brown sack, then we crawled the ladder and jumped in to pack the wool. When the sack was full we would surface on top. We'd get dirty, oily and full of ticks from the fleeces. About 5:00 PM the shearers would say, "We're quitting to go home, we got dates tonight." We thought they were swell guys to quit early so we could also. Dad thought dark was quitting time.

Joan took a job in Hisham, Montana teaching school. The harvest was good that year. We took a trip to the hills to take her some

Going to the Badlands.

Joan took a job in Hisham, Montana teaching school. The harvest was good that year. We took a trip to the hills to take her some winter clothes. We went this time by way of the Badlands. The unbearable, scorching sun quenched the beauty of it. We were hot and pathetic, with 4-40 drive, 4 windows down and 40 miles an hour. It was far less than a favorite memory. The Indians had named it well, the Badlands. When we got to Hustead's Wall Drug it seemed like an oasis. The ice water and soda fountain with flavorful ice creams revived us. We took pictures of the huge dinosaur and bought a petrified wood paper weight.

Chapter 21

Katherine Knippling and I would have long girlfriend talks. She had a way to interact with others. She had a corner on clues and cues of other human beings. As she matured, she developed a peer process which made people attach and attract themselves to her

Katherine at school.

Sister Roswitha

care giving manner. She was anxious and automatic about her goals. She seemed to know the requirements and manner in which to coddle her needs.

As a young girl she was anxious for new changes. She was the first one around to wear peddle pushers. Her father did not relent to this idea easily. She seemed to have remarkable power over him. When it came to learning how to drive the tractor and jeep, even though the jeep went through the fence while she was at the wheel, he stayed calm. She wanted to fight prairie fires with her father and the rest of the men. He was really tormented with the decision to allow her to do this. He said, "Girls shouldn't be out around the men, they might get ideas." But she overcame that with all the right reasons. A helping hand was always needed outside the home. She was a very capable homemaker at an early age. She would be flipping pancakes for all the 12 or 14 people around the large table at 6:00AM, when most teenagers were still in dreamland. She'd wake up to work. Early maternal biology. Not only was she growing tall, she had dimples that dented the whole cheek. She had blonde beautiful hair that needed no bleaching or touching up. Beauty without Vanity. The family of 9 children had parents that loved them equally, but she was never on a waiting list for that. She was a social leader of the girls at school and a good friend to me. The nobility and huge ranch her family had charmed and carried a lot of clout with the Nuns in High School. Once when I was called to the office for disciplinary reasons, I said as I walked in, "I'm Katherine Knippling today." Sister Roswitha looked over her thick glasses and with a rather scornful scowl said, "Sure you are." In spite of her great character she was never conceited. She carried her tall body with poise and competitive zeal and dreamed of becoming a movie star. She read True Confessions and True Romance magazines, yearned for romance and lived a fantasy for a few hours. Her feelings were electric and yearning to explore. She had the natural beauty and looked great even when she had just showered and her hair was dripping, tangled and sticking tight to her head and neck. When she smiled her gleaming white teeth complimented the deep dimples. She and Margy received many packages from home and always shared them. We would munch chocolate chip oatmeal cookies and huge frosted cinnamon rolls. We would discuss news from home while listening to the record player. I would be flushed faced from playing tennis, basketball and running. A mark of rebellion. Her feminine perspective was opposite of mine. But we appreciated each others individualism and western culture. She always inquired about my family and always asked about my sister Janet who had a bout of Rheumatic Fever.

At that time Ross would carry her to and from the car, when going to the Doctor. She was much too weak to walk. The snow was deep that winter, roads hardly passable but church was rarely missed. Ross and Janet became close that year. Cribbage, Canasta, and Checkers passed the long winter nights for them. No community dances were held in that sort of weather. Katherine would disguise her questions about Ross but she seemed to have feelings of interest. He had several girlfriends and perhaps she would be one some time soon, if she met with his approval. We shared many hours talking, laughing and discussing boys. She went home from school every two weeks and loved seeing her brothers and sisters. We were both letting our hair grow. No poodle cuts for us. We wore saddle shoes and liked jitterbugging and music by Kay Starr, Patti Page, Rosemary Clooney, Sammy Kaye and Johnny Ray. We enjoyed the songs, "Let Your Hair Down" and "Cry". Elvis Presley was a Pop star at that time. We wanted to see the movies "Seven Year Itch" and "Picnic" with Kim Novak. We had satisfaction knowing that we would see each other in the summer at church and dances. We had a mirror friendship that reflected a lot of each other.

The Sundance.

I told her about Art class. Sister Leonardo had a note on the blackboard, "Class, work on your projects, I'll be late today." We were learning about colors and mixing shades. Some of the girls had a special talent for doing this. We had painted gourds and some were drawing still life of a large bowl of colorful gourds. The students were in an inactive state. I jumped up on a long table and said, "You shake the gourds and I'll do the Indian Sun Dance that I saw at the summer POW WOW at Fort Thompson. You listen for the squeak of Sister's shoes." Every step that Sister took her shoes would squeak on the polished marble floors. The students' radiant smiles spread as I performed my reminiscence of the Sun Down Dance. They chanted and laughed but soon we heard the cue of Sister coming. We became motionless shortly before she arrived, announcing a QUIZ.

We often discussed whether each of us thought we missed a lot of fun by going to boarding school. Football, school parties with boys, we decided it was a trade-off. We were getting lessons in the real meaning of life, to have open minds, loving hearts and be charitable to all. We were obtaining a great deal of knowledge. Katherine said, "I think there would be fun anywhere you happened to be, if not, you would make some." We often shared ways that we were alike. Both Daddy's favorites, both born third in the family, both lived on ranches, both born in the 30's, both bright and inquisitive and wanting to enter "Man's World." We both started our education in rural schools, and we both went to Mount Marty. But there were ways that we were different. I was small boned, dark complexion, brown naturally curly hair and brown eyes. I grew up on the Reservation at Stephan, a small tight community. I went everywhere with Dad. Katherine was tall, blond, blue eyed, dimples, a Dutch hair-cut. She grew up with a lot of relatives in wide open ranch country. She wasn't allowed to go with her Dad. She had big responsibilities early in her life, making meals for all the ranch hands. Her heart was filled with kindness and she was yearning for a boyfriend, perhaps a cowboy, someone so exciting it would disturb the soul and he would support her well. She was ready to graduate, very anxious for the rest of her life to start. That spring went by fast, graduation was very near. Katherine's family would come and take her back to the ranch of wide open spaces. She wasn't distracted with going to college, although her grades were college material.

The summer of '51 we worked hard and goofed off, too, at dances and wedding Chivaris were often with several young people

103

getting married. The kegs of beer flowed and young people established identity with one another and emotional link for others. Some were memorable moments of first dates, others took on relationships that developed under pressure and quick marriages. At one of these happy times Katherine became Ross's girl. She was tender, appealing, beautiful, and electric. He

Katherine from first communion to high school graduation.

took powerful strides in his Lee Riders worn snug and faded, white starched shirt, custom fit Leddy boots, and Stetson roper hat. His attire suggested power and lusty rugged persuasion.

The two of them dancing made him perspire. His chest taunt and his Lee's were snugging his manliness. Her lips were warm, rosy, and smiling with happiness. She felt his eyes on her body, her long legs were next to his, her perfume compelling. The were joined in the moment. Would they have a legacy in the future, she was a woman desperately in love with Ross. It started as a child. She and he were raised with a firm hand and strong sense of morals. The test was now approaching.

Fall of 1951

Dear Folks,

I started this a month ago and didn't finish.

It was a fall night, the stars bright and twinkling, and there was a stream of Yankton boys in cars coming up the hill, driving up and down as if to torment the girls held within the walls of the school and gloating about their freedom. The fourth floor windows were lined with careening, vibrant, bright coeds. A black car stopped directly under the front entrance. Two typical expressive guys leaned out the window and broke the silence. "Come on Sweeties, have a night with us, you'll feel better in the morning." I responded to that with a basketball sized watermelon, from the Nun's garden. I held it in my hands, Margy opened the screen and with an instant great profile and a smile I heaved it out the 4th floor window. The hit was perfect. The upper level dormitories were laughing their asses off. The remains of the mess brought smiles and chuckles as the coeds filed by on the way to early morning mass. Most knew who. When I passed by I held up my open missal to hide my guilty, laughing face.

The way it is snowing here, and there also, according to the news, I'm wondering about getting home for Christmas. I'd have a sad, sour face if I had to stay here over the holidays. With all this snow I hope the spring thaws will not cause any problems for you.

Will write later.

Love,
Betty Jean

Spring 1952

Dear Mom, Dad, Ross and Janet,

Thanks a lot for the sweet chocolates with fudge centers. When we went to the Rec. room for recreation, guess what we had? Hot cocoa. Hope my complexion can handle all the chocolate. One of our classmates left school a week ago. She was a day student, about five months pregnant. They didn't say much about her only that she will no longer be a classmate. She didn't have body wisdom in advance.

I had a rather annoying attitude the other morning in biology. Sister Cyrilla always asks if we went to mass that morning, that's the first test question each day. She watches us with piercing looks. Then the question she asked me I thought was irrelevant to Biology. "Betty Jean, what do you do on a date?" That brought stares from all my peers. I was very present and connected when I answered. I looked at her and said, "Why, Sister, are you going to start dating?" The students just exploded with laughter. She did not look forgiving. Like never before, I wished I wasn't where I was. The disturbing statement may draw me an F. I will object to that manner of discipline. She pinched my arm as I went out the door in disgust.

At the 1952 Prom. Left to right, Anna Marie Winbauer, Clarence Courtney, Phyllis Yeoman, Lavern Stevens, Betty Jean and Art Hasker, Jr.

Remember the time I told you about Art Hasker that I thought was pretty swell. They have Hasker's Market. Well, I talk to him on the phone and when we get out on weekends we ride around with him. There are others along, Pee Wee Holter, Lavern Stevens, and once in a while we see Joan and Leona's friends, Jerry Frick and Jerry Pike. There are lots of guys that caravan up here. Anyway, we have these tickets we buy in the fall to go to concerts and symphonies. Everyone was talking about this great Mario Lanzo, famous Italian singer that they were so hep on going to. This Art Hasker gave me an option, "Let's go to Jan Garber at the Shore Acres Pavilion in Sioux City." I love dancing so the escape began. I was so excited and we had hand to hand joy as we danced. You know when you are with someone you enjoy, the hours flee like minutes when you have a passion for fun. This was happy, alluring and innocent but the clock ticked by faster than we could drive back. I definitely had a curfew violation. So when asked, surrendering was the most courageous thing I could do. When Sister said name a song that Mario Lanza sang, my distress was visible. I just shocked her by saying, "He's not my interest. I went to Sioux City, danced to music by Jan Garber and we dashed back." She looked duped. Perhaps if I said went to the Blue Moon Drive Inn and ate greasy fries and drank Coke, it would have been better. If only I would have known his hit song, "Be My Love." Then I said, "You know I am 17 and hug starved here, and please don't misinterpret that. You know, lack of affection may cause loss of appetite, which I could stand." She seemed never to bear a grudge and laughed at my comments. She let me know life was lessons. I embraced it with my wild spirit. Affection was scary to her for she was in a responsible position for us. She understood me better but objected to this episode. She let me know I had an unfailing sense of humor but this occasion was unappreciated.

The girls want to wear shorts or cutoffs and suntan on the roof. They want our bodies covered up.

My mind is escaping back to the ranch. I was thinking of the day Ross asked me to hand him that white flour sack with his books in it, when he was breaking the bay gelding. The horse was scared to death. We had a brief rodeo. Have you gone to Burkis' to see their new colts? Bet Albert and

Sarah and Lois and Wayne would like to show them. Wish I was there to go prairie dog and coyote hunting and have one of those thrilling rides in the jeep over the hills and down the ravines and across the prairie. My blood needs some excitement. Yeah!

Love to All
Betty Jean

P.S. How's Joan, the school mom?

The 50's times were changing, rural areas were getting the (the magic box) TV's. They were greatly improved, the programs were comedies, I Love Lucy, Jackie Gleason, Red Skeleton, and Ed Sullivan. The westerns were strong competition, Gunsmoke and Wyatt Earp. We all had our favorites, Art Linkletter's House Party had the day time viewers in his grip with his entertaining participants from the audience. The public was attacking high taxes and inflation. Eisenhower was running against Harry Truman for President. In 1953 he won the election. Truman did his best but it took years before it was realized. The health insurance was a new program. Most people didn't understand it at first. The Highway Act was the largest public work project. It gave thousands jobs, doing the nationwide Interstates which beefed up the auto industry, shipping and travel. The balancing the budget was promised and already an issue with debates as was segregation and discrimination. Newspapers carried the issues and problems of the nation.

Fashion was T-shirts, rolled up jeans, full dress with crinoline under skirts, tube and sack dresses were a disaster. Hair cuts were Poodle to pony tails. It was a rather cautious generation. People were wanting better jobs and more conveniences. Magazines carried ads for all the latest developments. People's *want* list grew and so did the competition among neighbors. The quote "Keeping up with the Jones' " came about. Socially the people went out to clubs and drive-in movies were big drawings for the younger set. These changed the neighborly camaraderie. The future was huge, exciting, and unknowable. The ambitious industries were buying, building and accumulating. Going on to higher education was being promoted.

The winter of 1951-52 was remembered for all the snow, blocked roads, and the continuous ground blizzards. People were anxious

The winter of '51 and '52.

the sun and the season to change. In March, roads were still snow packed. Katherine was working at the Bottcher Oil Company. She hadn't seen her folks for weeks so when they called in needing gas and fuel oil, she asked the truck driver, Oliver Stoley, if she could ride along to Knipplings and see her family. The roads were nearly impossible. Her dad had

used a Caterpillar to make the last miles clear. They had a welcome brief visit and some coffee and were on their way back to town. They had gone 3 miles when Oliver dropped over the steering wheel, the truck slid out of the track, Katherine didn't know what was happening. She was not for sure but needed someone to help. She ran back

Snow in '52—Lambert opening road for gas man.

109

to her parents, scared and out of breath. Her eyes were brimming now with tears as she whispered, "I think Oliver just died of a heart attack."

That spring the floods were dreadful. It was a statewide problem. The devastation to southeastern South Dakota and areas of Nebraska and Iowa was horrendous. From this disaster evolved the huge earth rolled Oahe Dam for water diversification and flood control.

Chapter 22

The summer of '52, Van bought more land, we would be total cattle ranchers. There was only slight grief when selling the rest of the sheep. The sheep herders were growing up. The $1600 for the quarter of Abe Lounder's land could keep me from going back to Mount Marty. I was happy and sad both. The attending private school was Dad's idea, he wanted the best education for his girls. He also gave the lectures, he would say in a serious tone, "You have one reckless night out, it can change your life." He put it well, we knew what he meant. He reviewed these lectures of discipline often when we'd ask to go to dances or dates. Remember beer will loosen your hunger for love, it brings out the male manner in men. You have to have boundaries. We could not ignore his words of gripping advice, it attached to my mind. He sat with ease, then let us go but with definite time to be home. He preferred we went in groups and not have any side road experiences. "Oh Dad go listen to the Joe Louis fight, we want to go out in the night and dance!" At times, we went to Stephan where Andrew Sargeant's band played (he was Lucy's son), or to Ree Heights, St Lawrence, Miller, or Highmore. We were hearing about places like the Chateau, Silver Spur, and Hopscotch where they had

Go-Go dances in Fort Pierre. We were underage yet. They were for the mature.

So came the transition of going to a different school when I was a senior. Everyone in a small town knows each other, so it was in Highmore. I missed the good school, students, and yes the nuns, would they be relieved and relaxed now? I was a chocaholic for a couple months. But Katherine was in town working so I would see her. We shared feelings and facts with some surprises. She asked if I missed Art Hasker Jr.? I told her we were pretty opposite, he's quiet, reserved, well mannered, but doubt if western life or attire would become him. He's joining the Navy. It was one of those laugh with a light hearted discussion that she said, "Ross and I are getting married the Saturday after Thanksgiving." It was as if her dreams were coming about.

She was elated with talk about her wedding plans. She would cherish every minute they would have. So as we walked to the door, I had to get back to school and her lunch time was passing, I told her then, "You know I met a flirtatious blonde blue eyed guy last night that's home from the Coast Guard. He has a black car that is fast as a rocket. He's warmly approachable, but Carol Wurts says he's been around and he's wild. His mother is Minnie, his father is Les, they run a herd of Black Angus cattle and farms with Sam and Bud Dancey. Years ago he lived on the Reservation until the drought caused them to move. They bought other land north of Highmore. His name is Merle Ankrum, he's nicknamed "Swede" because of his blonde hair and blue eyes. He's asked me to go roller skating at Orient. I haven't skated for years, the last was at the Stephan dairy barn, back and forth in front of the cows, so that may be humorous."

It was soon after that, my brother Ross pulled up when I was walking back from school. He said, "Are you going with that guy from up north that's out of the service, been around and rather wild?" And I turned and said, "Listen to whose talking. Besides serving his country which took him around the world with the Coast Guard, doesn't qualify Swede to have been around and wild! Besides, I have known him since I was four or five. I liked him when I didn't know his name. I saw him herding cattle and riding double, then he ignored me. Now he's making my heart skip. I like wild men like you and him." He drove off laughing.

We improved our skating, enjoying dancing and going to chivaries. Ross and Katherine's wedding was a large celebration, all

Ross and Katherine's Wedding. Ross, Katherine, Alice, Lambert and Nellie.

the neighbors came to congratulate, spend the day at the reception at the Knippling ranch. They looked so good in life that day.

The observing time began for Swede and me. I'd wonder if he'd have integrity, principles, and how would he look in thirty years or more, white haired and wrinkled from the prairie sun? Would we be important to each other in years to come? Right now he was a persistent image, usually close or on my mind. The honeymooners were back. The house was spacious so the bride and groom had the upstairs, Katherine was working in town yet. On one Saturday several trucks drove up. We wondered if they were lost. The driver said, "Lambert sent cattle for his daughters dowry." Nellie and Van looked out the door in dismay, "Whose custom is that?", Van asked her. Their future was looking up. The for better or for worse and with cattle!! In stark contrast to the $5 bill they found in the wedding card.

It was nearing the holidays which was such a festive time at Van Balen's. Van engineered the tree trimming, ordered the Dutch pastry with the almond filling from his family in Holland, and managed to find better hiding places each year for the gifts. Katherine loved the season, cooking fancy food and candy. Midnight Mass was tremendous, the music, the children's procession of those chosen to carry out the manger setting. Father Augustine, Father Alan, and the Sisters made the scene so awesome. The pews were packed, the back and the side aisles of the church full of Christians celebrating the

112

Ross Van Balen and Katherine Knippling on their wedding day.

birth of Jesus in a small, beautiful church. Indian and white folks brought their families for miles for this celebration. My friend Lucy always sat in the last pew on the left side, with her fancy black shawl with the fringe, she would acknowledge my smile to her.

It was soon after the Holidays that Mom said we should be thinking about what we planned on doing when school was out. At that time the choices were teaching, becoming a secretary or a nurse. The first two weren't even a consideration. Nursing, "maybe."

Going to town on a Saturday night was something we all looked forward to. It was lots of fun to shop at the big McLaughlin store. It was way ahead of its time, groceries, ready to wear, furniture, hardware and funeral coffins, all under one roof. The other stores, Home Grocery, Hamlins Clothing, Fairmont, the Theater and the beer joints all did well too. Later people would go to Rezacs or Nammanys Cafe to eat and visit. Kids would twirl on the stool seats and play. The parents would have all their needs for the week after selling eggs and cream.

Katherine would look forward to Saturday nights. The one evening as we walked along the street some old men were sitting on a bench. One said, "You gals know how many months it takes for a baby?" We never answered. He replied to his own question. "The

113

The bunkhouse, the first home of Merle and Betty Jean.

first one can come anytime, the second one takes 9 months." We walked on, but I said, "Why, John, are you counting?"

In the spring I didn't know the first step for a better tomorrow, but I trusted my gut. Swede (Merle) was digging right into my heart. He was healthy and fit. He had a great slim physique. He could have modeled western wear. We were having a great courtship. But summer was coming and as Mom had said, "What are you planning to do?" Joan was getting a job at the Reptile Gardens in Rapid City. Lee and Joe Campbell were opening the zoo at Custer. I thought I could do that. Graduation was marred with thoughts of going to work in the Hills the day after. At that time parents thought kids needed to get enlightened by leaving home to get a clearer focus of life. I should have known it would be similar to leaving for school, you don't know anyone, you are lonesome for your family and friends, and Swede had given me a diamond and wished I wouldn't leave. I saw him nearly every weekend which helped the dull week days. His idea of getting married in the fall was that he would build a new house within a year so the love story could go on to a story of family, land, and a Ranch. The schoolhouse and the bunk house on the north place told me I wasn't exactly going from ranch to riches. He was highly respected, his low voice of facts gave me encouragement. I couldn't find a better man to cherish. I had the Christian upbringing and faith and wanted to be accountable to it. My responsive convictions were profound on the day we recite our Nuptial Vows, then we shall become one. I will on that day wear my wedding veil down on my face as a sign to you of my innocence and virtues. We made plans for a fall wedding.

The big news in June was Katherine and Ross were parents of a big baby boy they named Clayton. The baby got so much attention from Nellie and Van. They cherished this baby. He grew up in a "Nuclear" household. Van couldn't wait to take him fishing. We were anxious for August so we could come home from work to see him.

Soon Katherine was back in her tailored western slacks, white blouse with black and white scarf tied around her neck. Her curves were back in the right places. When dressing in skirts and the Lucite high heels, with her hair pale blonde and bouncing, she was a beauty. She seemed so happy in the role of Mom. I was sharing with her my feelings and facts that I was enjoying these months of plans for the future and had no fear. We sat on the bamboo and leather furniture, and munched on chocolate chip and oatmeal cookies. I'd say, "I'm charmed by Swede, and he will love me forever. But I'm living the Monk regulations." We'd laugh lightheartedly. She said, "What about

Betty Jean and Merle Ankrum.

115

your wedding dress?" I said, "I'm going to Lucy's today and ask her to make a white velvet long gown." She had made me so many other clothes, that I wanted her to make my wedding dress. It would be so meaningful to me. So later that day I went to her house. There were several cars there, sometimes her friends would be there, but they seldom spoke to us, just looked, listened and laughed at times. Steve was outside. He said, "Go inside." They were cutting pieces for a star quilt, putting them in groups. I felt that the atmosphere was different. I asked her what I came for, "Lucy will you sew my wedding dress?" She looked rather hesitant and said, "I was in a car accident two days ago and not sure I would feel up to sewing that." They all kind of smiled. I said, "Were you out drinking fire water? Should I have stopped at the store to get popsicles to put the fire out?" The others covered their mouths with their hands and laughed. She said her other concern is getting something on the white velvet, machine oil wouldn't look good. I was rather disappointed but then she said she'd make my going away dress. I said I'd get doe-skin cotton and wish it were real leather. She asked if it was going to a big wedding? "Is your Dad finally giving you away?" The others were laughing wildly. They had real belly laughs over that. Then I said, "I'm inviting all of you to the wedding, and I'm never letting my Dad give me away. What does that saying really mean?" She said, "He is rid of you at last." They were laughing when I left saying, "Lucy Sioux Laughing Lady, you got the last laugh on me, but Dad's not giving me away. I am going and getting all of you

Betty Jean on her solo walk to the altar.

116

popsicles now." It was those kind of visits we remembered with laughter. On that visit she had everyone laughing. They would always grin at me in church. I didn't know their names, just that they were Lucy's friends. One was Ida Harrison, "Mrs. Smells the Earth", but the rest I couldn't call by name.

The day finally came. The church bells rang distinctly for the wedding. It was kind of rainy but the people didn't seem to mind. They enjoyed the togetherness. Mom had planned the house reception, made homemade buns and fixed ham. The tables were extra special with starched tablecloths and her bone china dishes. Friends helped her. I didn't have Dad give me away. But Lucy was there to see and smile. We had a hand and arm joy walk as we came down the aisle facing the new future, with many hugs, hand shakes and blessings from guests. The ceremony was over, the Indian school choir had sung so beautifully. We were ready for the romantic adventures that Father Allan spoke of and to which he had given his blessings, "Go forth like an olive tree and bear fruit." We were ready to taste and sample our new beginnings. Stimulated, sultry, desirous. Love was bonded. The honeymoon was 2 weeks through 14 states. We traveled and saw parts of the country unknown to us. I was a kid bride, starry eyed for a long time. We lived in the bunkhouse with a red Ford convertible sitting outside. You could tell from that, we were optimistic. I went with Swede to the Harrold place everyday.

Reception toast.

117

His Mother, Minnie, really taught me things I didn't learn at home, like making bread and how to have the whitest wash on the line. I had always been outside working at home. We didn't have phones at our home. Mom and Dad's visits were always a surprise. They would always bring a ham and a sack of flour. The didn't want us to go hungry. There were weeks that we ate popcorn for several meals.

Kids aren't for every young couple but as spring of 1954 came so did our symbol of love give me a new look. I had Katherine that would help me with all these changes. She was expecting her second child in June. I would have a fall child. Things were changing for us. We were building a new house but it wouldn't be done until winter. I couldn't wait, I would have running water and a phone, things I had been used to. Lucy sewed my maternity clothes and always commented about having little cowboys and cowgirls.

The TV promotion was beginning in the early 50's, but the booster stations were too far away. We went to movies like *Shane* and *On the Waterfront*. People were beginning to yearn for the things they saw in magazines and newspapers. The music companies were recording hits like, "Wheel of Fortune" by Kay Starr, "Tennessee Waltz" by Pattie Page, "Come On To My House" by Rosemary Clooney and "I Got Your Picture" by Patsy Cline. Sammy Kaye was my favorite band. So music and movies were our source of entertainment. Life was changing and they were dazzling years.

When September came our first creation was born. We named her Julie. She was a great first, most kind and caring for others. I couldn't walk for a week after her birth from stitches. Mom and Dad took me to their ranch. I was pampered and Julie was spoiled by Katherine, Mom and Dad for two weeks. When Swede came he said, "I'm too lonesome, lets go home." He had a certain softness that made being with him meaningful and easy. He said he would hurry and work longer days with Palmer Thingelstead, the builder of our house. Deadlines were not in our vocabulary.

The weddings were many. Joan was doing the planning for hers. She was moving to Des Moines where she had been attending Drake University. It is so hard to keep close contact when a family member moves so far away. It was a long days drive there. The phone would be our manner of keeping in touch. I had always appreciated her creative assets but I'd be far from her now. We would go see her in the summer because the winters were so harsh, with strong winds and blowing snow.

Many of the young families had baby "factories" going on. It was special to go to the Bazaar at Stephan the first Sunday of October and see all the friends and neighbors. We would spend the day enjoying good conversation and even moments of silence with each one, and reflect on the newest members of the families we hadn't seen. We had Jan in the winter. The roads were bad and we learned the meaning of a colicky child. She did everything early and got her first teeth at two and a half months. The colic left just as the Doctor said it would stop when she got her teeth. This child was interested in all things but horses were a priority. Some people had pets but we were having tots.

Wedding of Joan and Chuck Spain.

The area where we lived had many bachelors and the few neighbors were far away so it was very different for me. People didn't stand outside the church after services and share time with each other. The families that were far away were related so they spent time together.

Chapter 23

1957-1958

Katherine and I went places together, like going with each other to the doctor. These trips were times of sharing joys, triumphs and "name identity." I learned what that was all about. We rode in their wine colored Cadillac. The four kids would be in the back seat, Clayton, Craig, Julie and Jan. They always took toys along to pass the time. We would be gone 9 to 10 hours on the days we went to Huron. The order of business would be get the appointments done first, then we would shop in the retail stores. Katherine liked Larry's. The owner liked Katherine's family name and also her married name, Mrs. Van Balen. The store had high fashion clothes for women and also carried children's clothes. I was getting a full front with child number 3 on the way. Katherine was in the buying mood. Ross was cranking out a lot of money so though she spent wisely, money was not a problem.

A tall, slim clerk with dark bobbed hair approached me as I browsed in the little girl's department. My girls liked the shorts and tops they saw for spring. The clerk invited me to sit down and she would try the various outfits on Julie and Jan. After they had tried several outfits on, we decided on three. Katherine bought bunches and wrote a large check. When I went to the counter, off to the side sat Mr. Larry, the owner analyzing the purchases of each customer. I discovered I had only one check so asked if I could write the check for $25.00 more as we had not been to the grocery store and that was always good for $25.00. He had been like a quiet observer up to that point. He turned to me and said, "For the amount only, Lady." I said, "Keep your clothes and I'll keep my check." I walked out of the store. We bought our groceries and headed for home. Katherine would say, "Give me two aspirin and some water," and we would drive off into the sunset. We had four tired kids and two shopped out Moms. About 25 miles out of town, I looked in the back at the sleeping kids and was shocked at what I saw. I said,

"Look Katherine, that clerk never took those shorts off the girls!" She asked if I really wanted to go back. I said, "No, I didn't try the clothes on them so I'll chalk this up to Mr. Larry's name identity and what it can mean." We laughed and she thought he would be different to me next time.

Late 50's

During these years of the late 50's there were many area changes. Most people were having large families so of course there was need for the preservation of many food items. The neighbors all seemed to have freezers and then they started having Tupperware home parties, the plastic containers that sealed. Women had great social gatherings. At that time the topic of topless bathing suits brought forth many comments and jokes.

The cooking contests were new and many women had an interest. They were all creative cooks and the monetary winnings were an incentive.

Marilyn Monroe was in every magazine and picture pin-ups of her were of great interest to her many admirers.

While all these things were taking place, we were adding to our family. We had Julie and Jan and now a boy, (he was a night arrival). The doctor said he was a good looking boy but I was groggy from anesthetic and this left me silent for some time. The family called with congratulations and curious about his weight and name. He looked like a Pat to us. He brought humor and fun. Our house was getting very snug with kids.

Katherine and I would have many phone calls to each other if we weren't going places together. We discussed Liz Taylor, her beauty and jewels. The movie *Cleopatra* was out, starring Liz and Richard Burton. It was very entertaining with technicolor which added to the rich costumes.

Both families watched comedians Bob Hope and Red Skeleton. Westerns like *Gun Smoke* and *Have Gun Will Travel* would find us glued to the TV which had found its way into our homes. Katherine had a third son Todd that fall.

The hair styles were getting trendy with head bands and scarves. The guys had seams sewed in the front and back of their jeans.

It seemed like our amusement was having babies. It was the next year, 1958, on Easter Saturday that I had to trouble Dr. R. Jahraus.

He was dying Easter eggs with his kids, when he was called to deliver our second boy. Everyone thought we should name him Mike, even my Dad asked for that name, but I had heard too many Pat and Mike jokes. Perry and Pat were like twins they did have great times. Perry was a little more quiet.

Trips to Stephan to see family and friends at church continued. I asked Father Allen if he couldn't lighten that mystical blessing of "Go forth and multiply like the olive tree." We were going to need a castle for all the kids we were having. He focused on me with that broad dimples grin and said, "God is truly blessing your family."

Mom and Dad were making some changes. They were going to move to Highmore. Living in town would be quite an a adjustment. Janet would be graduating from high school and going off to nursing school in Huron. Katherine would miss the live in help with the little girl Carrie she just had.

Dad didn't know if it was right to plow the prairie. Farming was changing the landscape and also making ranchers a better income. Ross was giving his life meaning with the many avenues of income he was pursuing. He joined a corporation with four other men, John Heezen, Jesse Shaull, Gene DeHaven, and Elwood Redick to build a Sale Barn in Highmore. They also were very much in favor of the corporation that was building a bowling alley with a bar. The Sale Barn and bowling alley would be the social spot for the buyers and sellers. It was a fun place but tempers would flare and there would be fights at times.

Ross was making many encounters with cattlemen from Nebraska, Iowa and other areas. His life was full and lively with his love of Ranch and Beef but he was also acquiring a gut for scotch, which at times turned him into a maverick. His grip with a long moment handshake would often turn into a fist fight. I marveled at Katherine's ability to forgive. She would control him with her dimpled cheeks, smiling beautiful pearls gleaming, she would embrace him. It was an overwhelming example of what love can change. It was an unusual interaction but worked remarkably well.

Ross was soon ready for new ventures and horse racing seemed to grab his interest. It was something to take a chance on that intrigued others. The jobs on the largest earth rolled dam at Pierre were putting money in peoples pockets. The pay was very lucrative so betting appealed to many. He bought two Thoroughbreds named Lady Bardala and Ready to Rob. That Lady had winning legs. Francis

Knippling, a brother-in-law of Ross, had Vanzi Bar. He was tough competition and was raising many horses as was Pat Cowan.

Left to right—Jesse Shaull, John Heezen, Gene De Haven, Ross Van Balen.

1960's

Jim Easlands Alfa-Con feed processing plant in DeSmet had salesmen stressing the values of a high protein balance. Jim McAdaragh came to show Ross the value of such feed so he bought it for his race horses. He was sure the feed helped the horses win many Multi State races. When his horse was a winner, Ross would suggest they all go to the Spur Bar for refreshments. That was a popular place. They had strong drinks and loud music. People would try to imitate Elvis Presley, so there was a lot of wild shaking going on. It was one of those nights that Katherine and I went to the Cowgirl's room. When we returned there was a brawl going on. Swede wasn't in sight but Ross was. He was holding his bloody mouth and minus a tooth. Blood was covering the huge ornate Black Hills gold ring that reached to his first knuckle. There stood my only brother with a very disturbed look and fighting mad. I looked at him and said, "Gee, what happened?" He said, "That SOB was in my space and I told him if he got any closer I'd piss in his pocket!" The man reacted strongly. Too much Scotch often changed Ross's manner. I asked what Mom would say. "You won't be able to be the Marlboro man now." He had flushed cheeks as we filed through the crowd to the door and he wasn't sure that he wanted to leave. Others continued to slosh their drinks. Someone handed him his silver monogrammed cigarette case that had flew out of his pocket during the exchange of words and fists. The owner would have been wise to keep the music playing. The breaks were when the chairs and fists would fly. But those happenings intrigued people to return. It was a Western Combat Country Bar.

Chapter 24

One morning in 1960, Dad tried to get up early, as he always did, to take his diabetic test. He fell against the bed and dresser, and this awakened Mother. He could not get up, nor could she help him. She called her neighbors, Lien Marso's, for help. The ambulance took him to St. Johns Hospital in Huron. The doctor's preliminary exam showed that he had suffered a slight stroke, perhaps paralyzing one side.

March 9th, 1960 on a real wintry, snowy day, Father Mardian called to say he had been to the Tournaments in Sioux Falls and on the way home he had stopped at the Huron Hospital to see parishioners that were hospitalized. He was emphatic when he said, "I stopped to see your Dad. He didn't look a bit good. His face was very flushed and was breathing hard. I think you should get right down there." I said that when the snowplow gets through to open our roads we would leave immediately. I called Katherine to pass the information on to Ross. Their roads were open and he was anxious to meet us and go on to Huron. I said I would have to stop at Mom and Dad's house first. And to his question, "Why", I answered that none of my clothes fit very well. I had child number five on board and needed to pick up the maternity outfits that Lucy had made for me. He chuckled and said, "Swede and you are delicious lovers." I guess five under six years old proved that. I changed clothes very quickly and we headed for Huron. Ross drove very fast and on the way gave me instructions not to carry on like I had the last time Dad had been hospitalized. When I walked in and saw all the monitors with lines attached to him, I burst into sobs. I knew that I should have composure this time. My hands were gripping tightly in my pockets. Walking down the corridor, we arrived at the nurses station and they gave us his room number. When we got to his room, the door was shut and a man was sitting in a chair by the door. He said, "You can go in." Ross opened the door and we walked in. But the greatest shock was seeing the sheet pulled completely over Dad's face. I was looking in dismay at Ross and told him that I was going to pull the sheet back and see Dad. His face was very red and he was lifeless. I could not hold back my sad emotions. A head nurse came in, apologizing that we were not told at the desk or at least caught before we had entered. She said, "He died an hour ago." Mom and Janet had left to go to Janet's room at the Nursing School. It was our first immediate family death. I had to have time to realize that he was no more.

The Ankrums.

The funeral venture and the wake were new to us. We took all four of the children, Julie, Jan, Pat and Perry. Pat and Perry were very small, so they stepped up on a stool to look in at their Grandpa and almost in unison said, "Papa, have you got some gum?" Tears and smiles covered that statement.

The cemetery procedure seemed so final with the 7 gun salute. The sharp crack of the rifles echoed across the frozen prairie. The family held on to each other as tears froze to their cheeks.

The shock, with much grief, lasted for months. His Father in Holland, we were told later, had a premonition that day that something had happened to his American son Van. The news got to him a week later.

In a few days I helped my Mom take Dad's clothes out of the dresser drawers and closet. The deed was most difficult. I used a tea towel for a hankie. Piece by piece we boxed his things as friends stopped to convey their sympathy over a cup of coffee. Even writing about it 35 years later makes tears run down my cheeks, thinking of the family love we had shared. It taught me the values of the past, a precious legacy we pass through the seasons of life cycle. Now I knew the sorrow and deaths meaning. We missed that robust laugh, the excitement of making plans for Christmas, growing the flowers, sharing the wine and all his endeavors he had left behind.

Van Balens Coat of Arms.

The days went on. Mom got a grip on herself and went to renew her school teaching certificate. I had a baby girl, Vanessa, that summer. She had naturally curly hair and was idolized by her two older sisters, Julie and Jan and tormented by her two older brothers, Pat and Perry. Dippity Doo was new then and her sisters gave those curls a slick gooey look.

Once again Mom taught school. She did this for 5 years. I do regret never having gone to one of her Christmas programs. Folks wore their best clothes and the school was filled with happy, merry parents and children. The green curtains would open and the youngsters would perform like stars. The skits and music would warm their hearts, then Santa would come and the children would be so excited. He entered the gas lantern-lit room with his "Ho Ho Ho." The teachers gift to the children was a small brown sack of peanuts, hard candy and chocolate Bon Bons with white creme centers. Such a treat. Everyone had popcorn balls and sandwiches. The parents would have coffee with cream and sugar. Sometimes many Christmas songs were sung by all. These were treasured pasts.

People were eager, honest and hard working. They were open to the new changing life styles which were coming about. It was a time of new distractions. The war in Vietnam was on. We saw men with long hair, women in short shorts or hot pants. Dr. Spock was telling us how to care for our babies. Divorce, that was seldom heard of, was getting more prevalent. Foods of interest were yogurt and bean sprouts, whole grain breads and growing your own herbs. We began to hear about smoking pot. The movie industry was booming. Dr.

The Ankrums.

Zhivago and Butterfield Eight were hits. "Moon River" and "Rambling Rose" were favorite songs. The British Beatles were invading the country with their new style of music. Loretta Lynn, Patsy Cline, and Rosemary Clooney were belting out tunes like, "Coal Miner's Daughter", "I Fall to Pieces" and "Sweet Dreams." Cosmetic make up home shows by Mary Kay were becoming very popular. These shows taught skin care and how to become glamorous by applying makeup. Mary Kay offered great prizes in a multi-level marketing business. The consultants could win cadillacs, trips and other prizes. Katherine and I both knew we'd want to be consultants sometimes. John F. Kennedy was President at that time and was getting things moving. Businesses, large and small were profiting.

Women were getting remarkably pretty and their clothes were well designed. Leather with fringe caught Katherine's eye. The jacket she had was divine on her and public appreciation was shown with a stare, wink or whistle.

Cars were beginning to attract the youth market. Ford came out with a sports car, then a 2 seat sports car called the Mustang (named

The Ankrums.

128

after the wild horses). It not only got you where you wanted to go, but in style.

Toy cars were little boy "wants" as was Barbie dolls for little girls. On TV the kids liked to watch *Captain Kangaroo* with Mr. Green Jeans, *Ding Dong School* and *I Love Lucy*. Social significance was in speedy development.

Janet was just getting out of nurses training, taking her board and getting married to Jerry Venjohn. They were moving to Colorado. She had much to do in 6 weeks. I could help her with a ring bearer and flower girl but my defining symbol of love was showing and could not be disguised. She had Katherine and her friend Donna Jean Baloun as her attendants.

I never thought I was contaminating my body with any toxins but as we neared Thanksgiving, the doctor was saying, "No traveling." We had planned to go to Rapid City to my Aunt Monica's wedding. I was told to stay close to home in case I had to be induced. He was concerned with edema. We agreed with his wisdom, and when Vance was born, the doctor was not only a physician but a comic. He said, "I'll tell you what, I'll give you your 10th child free of charge." I said, "Don't count on that. I would like to see my toes the rest of my life instead of my belly." So here is boy 3 and I have 3 girls. We will rhyme his name with Vanessa and call him Vance. I hope people think when saying their names that I have 3 sets of twins, Julie and Jan, Pat and Perry, and Vanessa and Vance instead of 6 under 8. Vance was a grand little kid. If the other kids didn't entertain him he entertained himself. At a very early age he wanted to be a doctor.

Each time another child would go off to school, I would be rather lost and my spontaneous generosity

Janet and Vanessa. Janet's wedding day.

129

to giving new life was waning. Besides the house and car were full. Vance was one that loved to be rocked so after dinner I would watch "As the World Turns" and rock him.

Ankrum
Brand

Chapter 25

The winter of 1963 we had been married 9 years. We were like weavers, weaving shapes, six little children's shapes were now around our table. We were giving them a Christian contract, grace, love and western culture. Ranching is what we knew. If we should leave, it would seem as though we had lost something out of our soul. The wind blew a lot on the flat land. The rains would come up and then split and we'd get only a few drops when we needed a cloud burst to counter the drying winds. Many times we prayed for rain so the grass would hold up for the cattle. The children had only Swede (Merle) and my influence. We didn't want anyone to mess up out prize possessions. The Grandparents came on occasion. They had a house full of playmates. The neighbors were mostly bachelors, 11 of them. Merle wanted a winter vacation that year, so in February we talked about it, made plans, farmed the kids out to Grandparents and got in our '59 green Cadillac. Ross and Katherine were flying later to Mexico on a cattle buying trip, but Katherine said she'd love to jump in the back seat and go with us. She had uneasiness about flying in small planes. We would have liked their company. We went out on weekends to the Plains in Huron, the Chateau Steak House in Fort Pierre, where Pat Duffy had named a steak after Ross. They served him a steak and it was small, he called the waitress and said better take that back and tie two of them together. We would laugh, get wild, nuzzle, hug, and dance. It was those nights out that souped up our romance. It seemed as if we were flying to Texas, made it in

Card we got from Ross and Katherine.

11 hours. That Cadi gave a smooth ride and we got away from family and the land for a week.

The kids were passing out kisses and hugs when we got home and the real life story went on, broadening our scope of other places. The Grandparents were relieved and ready for release.

The spring came displaying promises of bumper crops. Katherine and Ross were making plans for the cattle buying trip to Mexico. They were going in a private plane. Katherine was telling us about their plans when we dropped in at Mom's in Highmore. She had her hair done at the Franklin Beauty Shop, by her favorite hair dresser, Valoris Huber. In Mexico, she would shop in the little villages for jewelry, baskets and pottery. Bringing surprises for her children. She would have fun selecting the gifts and enjoy the history and culture. The concern of getting sick from the food and water tormented her. She was trying to be optimistic about the trip to a warm climate where the sun, the flowers, bright colors and the bull fights would be a winter newness. She was nearly unstoppable as she prepared for the trip and to be sure of the children's well being during their absence. Todd and Carrie would go to her Mom's. Clayton and Craig were in school and would stay at the ranch with Nellie. She portrayed a happiness about living that was so remarkable. The look in her eyes was anxious but also joyful for everything life offered. Death was not an encounter of concern to this lovely 29 year old mother of 4 young children. She extended enormous love and support to those around her, cheering, giving, extending what was needed. Her life was fulfilled, stable and traditional with the luxury of those she loved around her. While enjoying life's lessons she became capable, clever and very individual. Her manner was one that could accomplish much in little time and was rather overwhelming to those watching. She was it seemed, so perfect. We often cheered each others work and endeavors. Adopted each others ailing house plants, share recipes that were sugar and cream rich. She was slender and never had to count calories. We could plan furniture arrangements and laugh at our endeavors. She was a beauty, proud, strong, striding and my best friend. Her work was well done, whether it be cooking, sewing, lovely table setting or gardening. Her beliefs were consistent and so strongly expressed to her God. Her hands were never idle. In moments of rest she would have an embroidery needle in hand, at night kneeling with her Rosary.

On the day at Mom's when she had her hair done in a beautiful French twist, I was so baffled because she and Carrie both were garbed in black. I remarked, "Why this black attire? I know the blonde hair against the black shirt and western pants is mystifying." The contrast was great, but Carrie, only 3, all in black too? She had not been to a funeral or lost any family member. We had tea with date filled cookies that Nellie made. Then she was going to stop at the

Carrie—"The Look Alikes"—Katherine.

132

Drug Store and get Dramamine in case she got sick flying. I had never flown so didn't know how that would be. She was happy, excited and we reminisced about things they would do and see, then we hugged a good-bye, "See you when you get back. Vance will be needing his baby shots, so could you go doctoring with me in a couple weeks? You can hold him when he gets his shots. You are his God Mother." She smiled her big dimpled, toothy smile and drove away, not aware of this important time we had shared. That week after they left for Mexico their son Todd had to go to the hospital with fever and a sore throat. Katherine had called her Mom Alice and was told of this situation. Knowing how shy Todd was, she became mindless about the vacation. Her concern was back with her family. She wondered if the pilot would fly her back to Pierre. Ross was not finished with his cattle business, so Saturday April 20, 1963, she boarded the 4 passenger, single engine, Cessna 172 private plane of Richard Runge. She bid Ross a final good-bye. The thought of seeing her children overcame the sadness of leaving Ross. The hypnotic drone of the plane's single engine could not drown out the fear. They flew by way of Denver and there they refueled. That day the Dakotas were having snow squalls. The pilot filed a flight plan at Denver, saying he would arrive at Pierre at 8:00 PM. He had fuel aboard to keep him airborne until 9:00 PM. The pilot followed the Platte River, the frozen vapors rising from

Ross and Katherine Van Balen's children, Craig, Carrie, Clayton and Todd.

133

the icy river waters hung ghost-like below them. The icy finger of death reached out to enfold them. At 8:30 the flight service heard an alarming call from Runge. He was unsure of his position. Hearing nothing more, search planes from a dozen Civil Air Squadrons in South Dakota and Nebraska were combing the rolling grassland and rugged hill country in a "recap" search mission. This was done after the FAA declared the plane and its two occupants missing. The CAP used 12 planes from Nebraska. Before noon on Sunday April 21st, Cecil Ice, owner and operator of a flying service in Pierre, spotted the wreckage. The plane was badly damaged but there was no fire. He landed his plane and found the bodies inside. He said that Katherine had beads in her hands. It was her rosary. Ranchers in the area told of hearing the plane circle for some time and then the noise suddenly disappeared. It had snowed quite hard in that area about nightfall. The CAP squadron at Valentine, Nebraska, said the wreckage was near the unmapped town of Bad Nation, just north of the Rosebud Indian Reservation. The spot is 23 miles east of the town of White River and just east of the graveled SD 53, visible from the highway. The bodies were recovered by sheriffs, deputies, motor patrolmen and Mellette County Coroner, M.E. Hiatt. Sunday morning, the FAA officials from Kansas City arrived at Rapid City to photograph the scene of the wreckage, 11 miles north of Wood along SD 53. Motor patrolmen stood guard. Ross was not notified for sometime because he was enroute to South Dakota on a commercial flight at the time of the search. She had not called him upon her arrival, so becoming very worried he flew home. He was grounded at Albuquerque because of bad weather. The FAA said it notified the airlines to inform Ross Van Balen of the death of his wife. The word of the disaster traveled like a jet. Our family was preparing to go to church in our best attire. When the phone rang, my grip became tense with the astonishing news. The traumatic news wounded our hearts. Thoughts of how to relate to this sad, tragic news numbed our spirit. I grieved so, for my dear friend. The day she wore all black, was it a foreboding of things to come? My mind rehearsed the last time I had seen her and Carrie. The stories were venerated.

Merle was asked to drive out to Rapid City to pick up Ross Sunday night. The snowstorm that confronted them now, snowing and foggy. The driving was dreadful, like driving in a tunnel of snow, everything hazy and wearisome. The trip was sad and very long. The one that would have made the most of every moment of such a trip was gone. I would have to see her to believe that she was no more. I was one of three to see her. At that time I could only imagine her agony with death. Her goodness moves me yet.

That Sunday Ross would never forget. His dream had been taken away because of a spring snowstorm. The depth of sadness was upon him. His heart was acknowledging but not accepting this hurting thought. He would never see his beautiful, tall blonde wife again. The loss would be of great magnitude. Her death would cause unbearable grief, along with agony and hardship. Regretfully he would recall his questionable behavior that had troubled her. He would remember those confrontations with no excuses. If only she could be with him now. Everything he looked at were things she had chosen and they all exemplified her. The plants, the magazines, the children's toys all neat, numbing his senses. They had clutched at happiness day by day. She had been tantalized by romantic notions. She got such an uplift from the man she had loved. He had whisked her heart away and now his heart was shattered. He grieved and prayed. Thoughts of joy and triumphs with her skipped in and out of his sad, silent sorrow. He sat by the window, tears rolled down his red weathered face. His slim stone body was sad,preverse, and silent. He removed the kerchief from around his neck. He could not remain in this isolated state. His children needed him. They had only him to be both Mom and Dad. He smoked a Camel cigarette and had a Cutty Sark drink but this did not help his grief. He knew he would carry her memory forever. He got up and began the process of the funeral arrangements, seeing to the children's well being. The "Running Cattle for Gain and Profit" would have to be put on hold. The window was a mirror of all the things they had worked for. There they were, cattle, horses, corrals, trees, fences, tractors, trucks and Cadillac. His noble wife, that had stood for all the things he cared about was no longer with him. Only memories. He wondered about the recurrence of deaths in the family. His Dad had lost his Mother and now two generations later it occurred again to his children. They were motherless. He felt powerless. Life here and after was a mystery but it gave him hope and perhaps he would be able to cope with this feeling of helplessness.

So on Wednesday morning April 24, 1963, the church and parking lot were over-flowing, as many friends, relatives and neighbors paid their last respects to Mrs. Ross Van Balen where she was laid to rest in the Stephan cemetery. The priest, Father Augustine, in his homily, likened her to a rose that God picked from his earthly garden when she was just beginning to bloom. The long procession of

The lifetaking crash.

people walking from church to the cemetery were teary-eyed, as the sound of an unknown private plane appeared and droned overhead magnifying the loss. There at the grave site stood Ross and the child-

Katherine

ren holding hands with cries of anguish outpouring. Carrie whispered softly to her Daddy, "Why is Mommy in a big suitcase?" Katherine, your position here is now over, I never told you, but thanks for being such a fine friend and part of our family. I will miss you forever, and now I will let go. The mourners assessed the sadness and pain they endured for the deceased. The view was implanted on my mind and will remain forever. Memories of Katherine live on so clearly to all who knew and loved her.

136

Where Have All Those Ranch Raised Kids Gone?

Katherine and Ross's Children

Clayton is a medical Doctor, married to Deb, has a son and daughter. They live in Green River, Wyoming.

Craig is a Doctor of Veterinary, married to Lauren. They live in Lexington, Kentucky.

Todd is a CPA, married to Kathleen, they have two sons. They live in Beaumont, Texas.

Carrie is majoring in Psychology, married to Randy Scott and they have two daughters. They live in Brawley, California.

The Ankrums

On the picture above from left to right:

Vance became a Doctor, married Tammie Van Eimeren, expecting a child. They live in Sioux Falls.

Perry works for the city of Pierre, married Sandy Peck and they have a daughter Abbie.

Julie is a 1st grade teacher and is working on a Master's Degree, married Rob Moncur, they have a son Brandon and live in Sioux Falls.

Pat has a Car Sales business, married Pam Felstad. They live in Boise, Idaho.

Jan is a counselor and is working on a Doctorate of Child Psychology, married Keith Ketterling. They live in Whapteton, North Dakota.

Vanessa is a Registered Nurse, works for St. Mary's Home Health Care of Pierre. She has a daughter, Lacey Jane, and lives on the ranch.

Merle and Betty Jean